"In this concise yet far-reach[ ] advocates for better societal a[ ] beginning with Christian churches. [ ] hand experiences and a wealth of statistics, Armstrong's critiques are trenchant and engaging. She also provides biblical stories to theologically reinforce her arguments that women deserve greater empowerment. With lean, practical prose, she easily demonstrates the Bible's message of equality and the deep influence of women on the history of Christianity. For anyone invested in uplifting girls and women around the world, Armstrong provides practical tips for getting involved. . . . A clarion wake-up call."

—PUBLISHERS WEEKLY

"*From Risk to Resilience* is the most comprehensive book in understanding the plight of women in the developing world that I have read. It is well documented yet accompanied by stories that help us understand the data. I was convicted and compelled as I read it. There are solutions, and we don't have to just shake our heads and feel guilty; we can be participants in change. May this be a clarion call to all who are followers of Jesus that what breaks his heart breaks ours. We will be part of the healing solution."

—JO ANNE LYON, general superintendent emerita and ambassador of the Wesleyan Church

"Jenny Rae Armstrong's *From Risk to Resilience* is a bracing exposé of the current global human rights crisis that is destroying and diminishing the lives of millions of girls. This crisis occupies a wide spectrum of expression—from the deadly sinister acts such as child marriages, honor killings, and sexual violence to more benign forms, such as limiting a girl's horizons simply because she was born female. This is urgent reading for pastors and ministry leaders, parents and teachers, and anyone who longs to see God's daughters flourish!"

—CAROLYN CUSTIS JAMES, author of *Half the Church* and *Finding God in the Margins*

"I'm so grateful to Jenny Rae Armstrong for this book. Her global research on violence against girls and women is shocking, but Armstrong doesn't leave us there. Through brilliant biblical exegesis, she corrects our vision and issues a practical wake-up call to the whole church, which cannot thrive without the presence of healthy women. May this book begin to turn the tide!"

—**LESLIE LEYLAND FIELDS**, author of *Crossing the Waters*

"*From Risk to Resilience* meticulously integrates relevant data, Scripture, and stories of change agents to show how empowering adolescent girls contributes to flourishing communities. Though the obstacles adolescent girls face are daunting, Jenny Rae Armstrong gracefully unpacks these challenges and equips her readers with tangible strategies for change. *From Risk to Resilience* is an important read for anyone invested in human thriving locally and worldwide."

—**MIMI HADDAD**, president of Christians for Biblical Equality International

"*From Risk to Resilience* is the most important book I've read in a long time, and it's a page-turner! Jenny Rae Armstrong weaves true stories of young women with well-researched statistics, Christian theology, and her own prophetic voice to call our attention to the ways that we, as a global society, must empower young women and fight for shalom. Read this book. You will grieve, but not for a moment without hope."

—**CATHERINE MCNIEL**, author of *Long Days of Small Things* and *All Shall Be Well*

"I'm committed to expanding my realm of reading in a way that reinforces what I care about most. *From Risk to Resilience* drew me in, deepened my understanding, and provided a biblical call to action. On the way, it equipped me to invest in women of all ages and in all places, that they might flourish and fully express who God has created them to be and what the Spirit has empowered them to do."

—**WAYNE SCHMIDT**, general superintendent of the Wesleyan Church

FROM RiSK TO Resilience

FROM RiSK TO Resilience

How Empowering Young Women Can Change
EVERYTHING

Jenny Rae Armstrong

HERALD PRESS

Harrisonburg, Virginia

Herald Press
PO Box 866, Harrisonburg, Virginia 22803
www.HeraldPress.com

Library of Congress Cataloging-in-Publication Data
Names: Armstrong, Jenny Rae, 1977- author.
Title: From risk to resilience : how empowering young women can change
  everything / Jenny Rae Armstrong.
Description: Harrisonburg : Herald Press, 2019. | Includes bibliographical
  references.
Identifiers: LCCN 2019003943| ISBN 9781513804095 (pbk. : alk. paper) | ISBN
  9781513804101 (hardcover : alk. paper)
Subjects: LCSH: Church group work with teenage girls. | Self-actualization
  (Psychology)--Religious aspects--Christianity.
Classification: LCC BV4455 .A76 2019 | DDC 259/.23082--dc23 LC record
  available at https://lccn.loc.gov/2019003943

Published in association with Books & Such Literary Management,
www.booksandsuch.com.

FROM RISK TO RESILIENCE
© 2019 by Jenny Rae Armstrong
Released by Herald Press, Harrisonburg, Virginia 22803. 800-245-7894.
  All rights reserved.
Library of Congress Control Number: 2019003943
International Standard Book Number: 978-1-5138-0409-5 (paperback);
  978-1-5138-0410-1 (hardcover); 978-1-5138-0411-8 (ebook)
Printed in United States of America
Cover and interior design by Merrill Miller
Cover photo: composite image using photos by Aleksander Kaczmarek and by
  Yaruta, Getty Images/iStockphoto

    All scripture quotations, unless otherwise indicated, are taken from the
Holy Bible, New International Version®, NIV®. Copyright © 1973, 1978, 1984,
2011 by Biblica, Inc.™ Used by permission of Zondervan. All rights reserved
worldwide. www.zondervan.com The "NIV" and "New International Version"
are trademarks registered in the United States Patent and Trademark Office by
Biblica, Inc.™
    Scripture quotations marked (NRSV) are taken from the *New Revised Stan-
dard Version Bible*, copyright © 1989, Division of Christian Education of the
National Council of the Churches of Christ in the United States of America. Used
by permission. All rights reserved.

23 22 21 20 19   10 9 8 7 6 5 4 3 2 1

For my grandma IrmaDel,
who embraced Jesus in everyone.

For my grandma Vivien,
who exemplified grace under pressure.

For my mother, Gail,
who broke the chains and showed me how too.

You scribed love, strength, and freedom
into every page of my life,
and I am eternally grateful.

CONTENTS

FOREWORD

Recently I walked through a rural village in eastern Congo with one of those brave souls who make the lives of others better—a public health doctor. As a physician, he had a thing or two to say about health, solutions to complex problems, and the nature of hope. Together we watched women dressed in the most brilliant colors wait with dignity as their children were vaccinated.

"You know," he said, with the fire of an evangelist, "women keep the world alive."

And he is right. Today in Congo, a country suffering from decades of war and the extreme poverty caused by conflict and greed, one out of every five children won't see their fifth birthday because of preventable diseases like malaria as well as malnutrition and diarrhea. But those who do survive owe their lives to mothers, sisters, grandmothers, and aunties. It is women and girls who make sure community water is clean, the family is planned for, neighbors are listened to, children are schooled, the community is vaccinated, meals are as healthy as possible, sickness is avoided, shoes are worn, teeth are brushed, and sleep and play are made a priority. Even in a war zone. *Especially* in a war zone.

Still, it is girls who are most threatened. The heartbreaking truth is, they are not *possibly* at risk of rape, hunger, infanticide, obstetric fistulas, slavery, sexism, and poverty. Girls are *probably* at risk. In fact, 100 million girls are missing because of gendercide. They were never given a chance to live.

Hard to believe. Hard to forget.

Turns out, violence against girls and women goes back a long time. Even to the Bible. This is why my friend and colleague Jenny Rae Armstrong says, "Get mad at me if you want." Armstrong fearlessly quotes Jesus, church fathers and mothers, the Bible, theology, history, and the lived testimony of women around the globe as she calls the church out of the pew and into the arena. Armstrong wants to start more than just a conversation; she wants to start a revolution.

A revolution of resilience.

Armstrong's voice carries the authority and compassion that comes from years of learning and teaching, fasting and praying alongside those who suffer. She unapologetically challenges us to search the face of God for the sake of the world's most endangered species—the human girl.

Armstrong has given us all the most generous of gifts in this beautiful book—motivation to know and care about the plight of girls and do something about it. Bottom line: when girls survive, communities thrive. After all, the resilience of girls will truly "keep the world alive" and flourishing.

—*Belinda Bauman, executive director of One Million*
Thumbprints and author of Brave Souls

Introduction

Twelve to twenty-one is the most dangerous age for our girls."

I was standing in a lunch line in western Kenya, the sun pounding down on my head as I waited for my serving of ugali, stew, and sweet, milky tea. I had traveled to East Africa at the invitation of the Ekklesia Foundation for Gender Education (EFOGE) to train the people who would be piloting the Bible-based youth curriculum on gender justice I had written. But I was the one who was getting an education. High school teachers told me about the unfair distribution of labor that had girls gathering wood, cooking, and cleaning while their brothers studied for qualifying exams. The archdeacon of the local Anglican diocese talked about how the sleeping arrangements for girls in their tribe made them vulnerable. A laywoman caused a minor uproar when she insisted that women wouldn't be treated as equals until the dowry system, in which women were exchanged for money or livestock, was demolished. And Rev. Domnic Misolo, the executive director of EFOGE, explained why they were focusing so much energy on reaching girls between the ages of twelve and twenty-one.

My heart broke as he talked about how adolescent girls in their community were circumcised, removed from their father's home, married off for dowry money, or lured into bad relationships in an attempt to escape a difficult home life. Poverty, polygamy, violence, and disease were scourges on their families, taking a special toll on women. But if girls could just make it through the difficult adolescent years—if they could put off marriage, finish school, and avoid getting pregnant until they were physically and emotionally ready to handle it—their chances of living healthy, stable lives skyrocketed.

Some of the stories rang strange in my Western ears, but others were all too familiar. We've all known the girl who got too serious too fast, because her boyfriend seemed like a better bet than her family. We've all known the young woman who got pregnant and dropped out of school, unwittingly locking herself and her children into a cycle of poverty. We've all known the one who got tangled up in an abusive relationship and didn't know how to get out. Maybe we were that girl, or maybe we were her father, mother, sister, brother, teacher, pastor, or friend.

These issues don't surprise us, but the fact that they are so universal should give us pause. What is going on in the hearts, minds, and lives of girls between the ages of twelve and twenty-one? How are our own actions and attitudes, and the actions and attitudes of the societies we live in, helping or hurting them? How can we empower young women to become agents of change, setting a better trajectory for themselves, their families, their communities, and the world we all share? Can we help them live out the apostle Paul's mandate in Romans 12:21 to not be overcome by evil but to overcome evil with good?

Gender-based violence, educational barriers, early child-bearing, and other common problems would be critical enough if they only affected the lives of young women, but the fact is they affect society as a whole. Development experts agree that educating and empowering women is the most effective way to combat extreme poverty, slash child mortality rates, stem the tide of HIV/AIDS and the orphan crisis, and build healthy, sustainable communities where people can live in dignity and safety. But first, women have to survive childhood and navigate the minefield of adolescence. Will they stay in school and improve their economic prospects, or partner off and have children they are unequipped to care for? Will they be trafficked to keep their siblings fed, or taught a trade so they can contribute to their family's well-being? Will their intellect, gifts, and passions be nurtured and encouraged so they can do the good works God has prepared for them? Or will their light be suffocated by the darkness determined to steal, kill, and destroy their body and soul?

That is what this book is about: the particular dangers that adolescent girls face, and what happens when they are given the mental, emotional, social, and spiritual tools they need to overcome those challenges. We'll also delve deep into the Bible, examining oft-ignored texts that talk about the issues that girls face, and we'll consider what God has to say about them. My prayer is that this book will equip all of us—parents, pastors, teachers, mentors, lay leaders, and friends—to become the cheerleaders and champions girls need, committed to their flourishing. May it be so!

ONE

Growing Up Girl

A PRIMER ON THE PROBLEM

She was pregnant. There was no denying it anymore.

It wasn't the baby she was worried about. She was actually kind of excited about that, although she had no idea how she was going to support the child. She'd cross that bridge when she came to it. No, it was the people in her village she was worried about—particularly the man her parents had promised her to. Would he show up on her father's doorstep and demand an honor killing when he found out? Or would she be publicly disgraced and sent away, cast out of polite society?

She did what countless girls all over the world have done in her situation. She came up with an excuse to skip town and took refuge with a relative in the city, where one more pregnant teenager wasn't likely to be noticed.

The story is as common as water. My maternal grandmother lived her own variation of it. Sent away from her small town to protect the reputation of the man who had raped her, my grandmother returned several months later as if nothing had happened. As if she hadn't been forced to hand a beautiful, red-headed baby over to the strangers who would raise him. Like countless young women of her time, she and her child were cared for not by friends or family members, but by religious workers at a home for unwed mothers. It was a much-needed rescue, but far from ideal. I wonder sometimes, driving by historic buildings that once housed young women with nowhere else to go, how many girls just like my grandmother walked in and out of those imposing doors. I can't imagine the terror they must have felt, pregnant and alone, facing a future where the only certainty was pain.

But these young women were not just victims. They were champions, bravely enduring an unjust barrage of shame and suffering so their children could have life. Chances are good that you have someone like them in the branches of your family tree—that you owe your existence to the stubborn courage of a teenage ancestress.

That is certainly the case in your spiritual family. When God launched his rescue plan to save the world, he didn't approach the high-born male leaders and invade with armies and fanfare. No, God chose a teenage girl named Mary from the backwater town of Nazareth as his closest ally, the one he would entrust his life to, and entered the world in the most ordinary, ignoble way possible.

That makes quite a statement about the value God places on teenage girls, and how God must feel about the world's low view of them.

TALKING TABOO

Polite Christian society often shrinks away from addressing gender-based issues. Oh, we may joke about how differently men and women think, or hear preaching on the roles our church assigns to each gender, or even have quiet conversations about domestic abuse or pornography addiction in women's or men's small groups. But the robust, brutally honest conversations we need to be having are more likely to happen on the Internet, in a coffee shop, or in the community meeting room at the local library than under the steeple. That is a tragedy.

It is also ironic, since the Bible does not shrink from stories about the violence, oppression, and lack of opportunity that stalk so many girls. Most Christians don't talk a lot about Sarai's slave Hagar, at least not in a positive light. We don't preach sermons on Tamar's disgrace or the rape of Dinah. We talk about Esther like she was a contestant in a beauty pageant, not a young girl forced into the harem of a tyrant who was stockpiling virgins. We forget that Mary was facing not only disgrace but the possibility of being stoned to death when she agreed to carry the Savior of the world. And we don't realize how significant it was that Jesus spoke with the Samaritan woman and defended Mary of Bethany's right to sit at his feet.

The stories of women and girls weave an intriguing counterpoint into the biblical narrative, often providing a scathing cultural critique. They remind us that as inspirational as Abraham, David, and other heroes of the faith were, things were not all as they should be. The sisters and strangers, wives and widows, daughters and slaves and concubines and mothers of Scripture testify that even heroes can behave like villains, and that culture has a long history of colluding with the powerful at the expense of the vulnerable. Those of us who believe the Bible to be the inspired Word of God need to wrestle with these texts, asking ourselves what God's purpose was in including those heartbreaking stories and what they have to say to us today.

A decent place to begin would be by acknowledging that things are not all as they should be today, either. That sometimes even godly people wind up colluding with the powerful at the expense of the weak, turning a blind eye to suffering, or even become so desensitized to the commonplace injustices of the society in which they live that they don't realize what is happening is wrong. That they don't bat an eye at mutilating their daughters' genitals, or selling them into marriage, or sending them away to protect a rapist, or limiting their opportunities because they are female. They might even think it is the God-honoring thing to do.

If we were to take a cue from the biblical writers and tell the stories of modern women and girls swept into the riptide of our global society, what could we say? And would we have the courage to say it?

WHAT IS A GIRL WORTH?

When Domnic Misolo, my colleague from Kenya, messaged me a picture of a baby girl, I was confused. I knew it couldn't be his child—at one and a half, the baby in the photo was too young to be his oldest daughter and too old to be his youngest. Domnic would occasionally send happy photos of the teens his ministry was working with, but this picture didn't fit the pattern. Was this the daughter of one of those girls? I didn't have to wait long to find out.

"This little angel was raped this morning by her own father."

My heart sank into my stomach, and I began to tremble.

More details followed. The girl's mother had gone to the hospital to give birth to her second child, leaving the toddler alone with her father. The father, who was HIV positive, had been advised to have sex with a virgin to get rid of the disease. The toddler was at hand, and the father did what he perceived to be in his own best interest. After all, his life was more important than the life of any girl, even his own daughter.

Blessedly, the mother went to Domnic for help as soon as she found out what happened. The child was started on HIV-preventative drugs, and money was raised to get her the life-saving reparative surgery she needed. The mother and her children were welcomed into her brother's home, allowing her to stand against the father's insistence that she drop the charges and move back into his home. Still, her options as a young woman without any marketable skills remain bleak.

This book is about adolescent girls, not babies. But if we want to get a good sense of the issues girls face, we need to consider them within their broader social context. The reality is that the core problem is not poverty, or violence, or any of the other issues we are addressing in this book. We can't solve it simply by rescuing trafficked girls or preventing teen pregnancy. No, the core problem resides squarely in the hearts and minds of human beings, in the ubiquitous devaluation of women and girls.

This devaluation is expressed in countless ways, large and small. It manifests in the belief that sons are preferable to daughters, that females exist for the benefit of males, that a woman's primary purpose and value is found in the role she plays in relationship to others. Some cultures are more circumspect about it than others, but there is not a corner of the globe where those pernicious lies about a woman's worth do not hold sway. And the problems those beliefs create do not hold off until puberty.

SURVIVING THE GENDERCIDE: ONE HUNDRED MILLION MISSING WOMEN

Before we can talk about female flourishing, we need to talk about female survival. It is true that more boys are born than girls, and it is also true that women tend to live longer than men. Taking those biological factors into account, researchers have discovered that close to one hundred million females are inexplicably absent—inexplicable unless you account for gender-based violence and neglect. In *Half the Sky*, Nicholas Kristof and Sheryl WuDunn explain that "more girls were killed in the last fifty years, precisely because they were girls, than men killed in all the wars in the twentieth century. More girls are killed in this routine gendercide in any one decade than people were slaughtered in all the genocides of the twentieth century."[1] The fact that these jaw-dropping statistics are not plastered across the front page of every newspaper and constantly looping on network news shows how numb we have become to the routine violence women face.

The danger begins in the womb. Sex-selective abortion has skyrocketed as technologies to determine sex and end pregnancy have proliferated. When pregnancies are allowed to run their natural course, approximately 105 boys are born for every 100 girls. When the sex ratio at birth goes above 108—that is, 108 boys for every 100 girls—researchers attribute it to abortion or infanticide, not biology.

While it can be hard to track down the exact numbers, particularly in regions where many women give birth unattended or do not report their child's birth, the gender gap in many countries is glaringly obvious. The United Nations estimates India's sex ratio at birth to be 111 and China's to be 118. The ratio is higher in urban areas, where abortions are more readily available—Vietnam's ratio is 111 overall but 116 in densely populated areas; Pakistan's ranges between 110 and 112. It happens in the West as well. Liechtenstein, a tiny Alpine country that has the highest gross domestic product per person in the world, also has the highest sex ratio at birth: 126. Armenia is an interesting case: the ratio is a staggering 138 among couples having their first child. If the first child is a son, the ratio for the second child drops to 85, showing a strong preference for an older son and a younger daughter. If the first child is a girl, the ratio for the second child skyrockets to 156![2] There are no natural means by which those numbers can be explained.

Abortion has largely replaced the ancient practice of infanticide, but it still happens. Female babies and babies with disabilities are especially vulnerable. The lucky ones are abandoned alive in a place where they are likely to be found; others are quietly dispatched, typically by their mothers. The problem is still significant enough that many nonprofits and government organizations have set up places where infants can be anonymously given up without social or legal consequences. One documentary features the "baby box" that a pastor set up in Korea to take in endangered infants. In Pakistan, babies are laid on the doorsteps of mosques. In the United States, newborns can be relinquished at hospitals and clinics and to emergency medical service providers.

Many states allow babies to be dropped off at fire halls and police stations.

Neglect is another factor in the case of the missing females. While 5–6 percent more boys are born than girls, girls are less susceptible to birth trauma, medical abnormalities, and common childhood diseases. All things being equal, girls are about 8 percent more likely to survive to age five than their brothers. However, in societies that value sons above daughters, girls are more likely to go without the nutrition, medical care, and other things they need to survive and thrive.

This is particularly problematic in China and India, which together make up 36 percent of the world's population. When those two countries are removed from the equation, 77 boys and 69 girls out of every thousand die before their fifth birthday. That is the average across all other countries, accounting for everyone from Canada to the Democratic Republic of the Congo. However, when China and India are added into the equation, male child mortality drops to 69 per thousand (thanks to the quality healthcare available in those large nations) and female child mortality jumps to 70. While the equality of those numbers sounds right on the surface—we don't want *any* boys or girls to die—it actually signals that something is deeply wrong. In fact, girls born in India are 75 percent more likely than their brothers to die before their fifth birthday.[3] If a girl makes it to age five, she often enjoys a slight respite until she reaches puberty. The issues she faces during adolescence will be addressed in the rest of this book.

But before we move forward, let's look back and see what the Bible has to say about how we arrived at this state.

IN THE BEGINNING

Genesis 1 may be one of the most astonishing pieces of literature ever written. In it, we are introduced to a creative, relational God—a God who brings the cosmos into being; who hovers over the dark, unformed chaos of the deep like a dove brooding over her nest; who opens his mouth and speaks light, and life, and blessing, proclaiming his creation good. Then comes the magnum opus, the pinnacle of creation: "Then God said, 'let us make mankind in our own image, in our likeness, so that they may rule over the fish in the sea and the birds in the sky, over the livestock and all the wild animals, and over all the creatures that move along the ground.' So God created mankind in his own image, in the image of God he created them; male and female he created them" (Genesis 1:26-27).

Chronology-obsessed Westerners are tempted to jump ahead here. We read chapter 2 into chapter 1, and visualize the 'adam—the man—of the garden standing before the Creator alone, receiving his blessing and his mandate. The woman will come later, we assume, and receive them by proxy through her husband. She is to be his "helpmeet" after all—his *ezer kenegdo*—helping him fulfill the awesome responsibility God has entrusted to him.

It's an understandable mistake, but a grievous one. There is a reason that chapter 1, with its cosmic story of creation, comes before chapter 2, which focuses in on a plot of earth, a vessel of clay, and the divine arithmetic in which one becomes two, and two become one. God wants us to get the big picture, to understand who God is and who we are in relation to God, to one another, and to the earth he placed us on. Both male and female are created in God's image. Both are blessed and told to be fruitful and multiply. Both are tasked with ruling over the earth as co-regents of God's creation.

It is important to note that God calls the man and the woman to rule over and subdue the earth and the creatures, not one another. There is no hint of hierarchy between the man and the woman in chapter 1; none of the power struggles, division, or trauma that mark so many male-female relationships today. Even in chapter 2, in the garden, the woman is presented as an equal co-laborer with the man. *Ezer*, translated "helper," has military overtones, and is usually used to describe God or a powerful military ally. *Kenegdo*, translated "meet" or "suitable," is a complicated word that implies equality and counterbalance, and simply means that the man and the woman correspond to each other.

Imagine a set of rafters: two beams joined together at the peak, holding up opposite sides of a roof. The rafters need to be made of the same materials, the same length and strength, able to support one another while holding their own weight. They need to be *kenegdo*. If they are not, the whole structure is in danger of collapse.

So what happened? Where did things go so horribly wrong?

UNDER THE CURSE

The downward slide begins in Genesis 3. In chapter 2, the man and the woman were placed in the garden, free to eat from any tree (including the tree of life) except the tree of the knowledge of good and evil. But they were not content. Deceived by the serpent and tempted by the idea of becoming like God, they sank their teeth deep into the illicit fruit, and nothing was ever the same again.

The rebellion of the regents God had appointed over the earth carried stunning consequences for their realm. Their relationship with God was broken, marred by sin and shame. Their relationship with one another was broken. The woman would now try to find her identity in relationship, and the man would now try to find his identity in power, creating a dysfunctional dynamic that was at odds with God's intention for them. The earth itself was broken, as were our bodies. Creating and sustaining life, from the womb or from the soil, would be painful and labor intensive, and eventually everything would die. The man and the woman were forced to leave the garden so they wouldn't eat from the tree of life and live forever in that sorry state.

Things got worse from there. A man named Lamech married *two* women. One was named Adah, which means ornament, and one was named Zillah, which means shadow. The "sons of God" took any women they chose. Humankind became so violent and depraved that God wiped the slate clean, sparing only Noah and his family—but still, humanity struggled. The Bible points us toward redemption, yes. But it also paints a picture of just how ugly humanity can be, and how desperately men and women need to be redeemed.

MISPLACED IDENTITY: IT'S NOT A PRETTY PICTURE

If you grew up going to Sunday school, you've probably heard the story of Queen Esther. When Queen Vashti, the wife of the notoriously unstable King Xerxes, declined to do a striptease for the king and his drunken noblemen and military officers, the king decided to upgrade to a younger, more pliable model. He appointed commissioners in every province of the Persian Empire to find and bring beautiful young virgins into his harem so he could take them for a test drive and choose the one who pleased him best to carry the title of queen. Esther, an orphaned Jewish exile who had been raised by her cousin Mordecai, was one of the girls taken.

Warned to keep her family history and ethnic identity strictly secret, Esther began the process of becoming whatever the men in her life wanted her to be. She ate the foods the Persians brought her. She submitted to the beauty treatments they prescribed. When it was time for her to be brought to the king, she did exactly as she was told. Like so many other women and girls throughout the centuries, Esther buried her true self in the interest of survival.

She even changed her name. In Esther 2:7, we see that her given name was Hadassah. It came from the Hebrew word for myrtle, a fragrant, resilient evergreen that grew wild on the hills around Jerusalem. The name Esther, on the other hand, had a double meaning that would define her life in the harem. Persians would have thought of the fertility goddess, Ishtar. Jews would have heard *hester*, the Hebrew word for hidden. Esther: the sex goddess whose true self was hidden.

Names are significant, as I mentioned with the case of Lamech's two wives, Adah and Zillah. While we cannot be sure why the author of Genesis made a point of sharing their names when biblical women are so often anonymous, the fact that their names are included makes a striking statement. The first woman in the Bible was named Chava, which means, simply, "living." (How we got Eve from Chava is a question for Hebrew scholars.) The second and third women named in the Bible were demoted to "ornament" and "shadow"—both of which, as identities, are a sorry excuse for living, as many women can attest. Not only were Adah and Zillah forced to share a husband; they were expected to bear witness to his violent behavior and presumably offer their silent support. They were, after all, Lamech's ornament and Lamech's shadow.

How did women fall so far, so fast?

If we flip back a few chapters, we can find a hint in Genesis 3:16: "Your desire will be for your husband, and he will rule over you." As members of the human race, women had been created to be fruitful and productive, to rule over the earth and creatures in community with men. Carolyn Custis James describes this male-female partnership as "the blessed alliance," in which men and women work together to accomplish their common purpose—God's purpose. But when sin entered the world, the relationships between men, women, and God became skewed. Instead of finding their worth, purpose, and identity in who and what God created them to be, women would find their worth, purpose, and identity in their relationship with men. This suited men, who had also fallen into sin, just fine.

While every human being has a deep, God-ordained need to be in relationship with other people, finding our identity in anything other than God is dangerous. We were made to be image-bearers: creative, relational beings who reflect God's loving care to creation in all our diversity. When we seek our identity outside of that, we inevitably have to twist, shrink, and contort our souls in an attempt to fit into our identity of choice. We put on a pleasant mask and become an ornament. We shuck our confidence and become a shadow. Lamech's identity was bound up in his concept of honor, causing him to boast about killing the young man who had wounded him. We're still embroiled in this demented game of charades today.

THE INCREDIBLE SHRINKING GIRL

We all struggle with our identity at times, but few do it as obviously as adolescent girls. A cheerful, confident fifth grader stops raising her hand in sixth grade. A bullied fourteen-year-old dons alt clothes and makeup like a suit of armor. A queen bee goes on the offensive, managing her life like a political campaign designed to keep her in power. The brainiac checks out, burying herself in online gaming. And that's not even mentioning the contortions that girls go through to make themselves attractive to potential romantic partners.

Experimenting with how we express our personality is a normal part of modern culture, especially in individualistic societies in which options abound. But when social expectations begin striking at the core of our identity, we have a problem. Many of these expectations are so ingrained in our culture that we have a hard time recognizing them, much less knowing how to deal with them effectively. We'll spend the rest of this chapter looking at three common false identities that cripple adolescent girls around the world: the Sweetheart, the Servant, and the Siren.

It is important to understand that the characteristics associated with these false identities are not necessarily good or bad. Think of them like photographs in a magazine—staged, shot, and digitally altered. Each presents an idealized version of womanhood and tells us something about what the society that produced that image values about women and girls. The pictures are, for the most part, morally neutral, and bear some resemblance to the real lives of real women (although with Photoshop, one never knows). But living, breathing girls can't squeeze themselves into a 2-D tableau of femininity without flattening their sense of self and doing violence to their souls.

This pressure doesn't come from the girls alone; sometimes it is their family, or friends, or church, or the society they live in that pressures them to conform to damaging ideals. Let's take a look at these paradigms, starting with the one that seems most benign: The Sweetheart.

THE SWEETHEART

One of the problems with discussing injustices against women and girls is that it can make it seem as if the whole world has it in for females; as if all of life is a zero-sum game of boys versus girls. In reality, most parents love their daughters and want what is best for them. We love our girls just as much as we love our boys, and we express that love in countless big and small ways.

But our ideas about what is best, and the ideas we pass on to our girls, often have more to do with human expectations than God's. Enter the Sweetheart, also commonly known as the Good Girl, Daddy's Girl, Mama's Helper, or Teacher's Pet.

"I felt immense pressure to live in such a way that no one would find reproach in my life," my friend Cheryl explained, describing how the Sweetheart identity develops.

These pressures came from my home, homeschool community, as well as the churches I was a part of. If anyone became upset or uncomfortable with me I internalized it as my fault because they could find something in my tone, body language or words that would bring reproach to God's kingdom. I remember stating once that I felt I could make most any man happy as his wife because I could accommodate others so well. And I was proud that I could be so accommodating! What I know now? I had learned to be nothing so others could be whomever they wanted—and I interpreted it as godliness.

The Sweetheart may seem—and may in fact be—happy and well adjusted. But her need to please the authority figures in her life serves as a tether, shackling her to expectations that may help or hinder her as she moves into adulthood. That tether serves a dual purpose for parents, allowing them to manage their daughter's behavior—which makes the family look good—and yank her out of the elements at the first sign of rain clouds—which keeps her "safe" and prevents the family from looking bad.

As a result, it is common for a Sweetheart to enter the world woefully unprepared for the harsh realities of life outside the protective cocoon in which she grew up. Some Sweethearts struggle through an awkward emergence and then soar, buoyed by the love and support they received as children. Others never stretch their wings, preferring to remain in a cocoon that doesn't really fit anymore but is comfortable and familiar and shields them from the things they have been taught to dread the most—struggle, failure, and conflict.

The failure to thrive that comes from the Sweetheart's tendency to stay within the comfort zone her family set for her is bad enough, but it becomes truly dysfunctional when the Sweetheart finds herself in a situation in which compliance is an inappropriate response. What happens when a young Sweetheart feels uncomfortable with the "affection" she is receiving from a man from church but the man is someone she has been taught to respect? What happens when her boss asks her to doctor a few numbers on the financial statements and assures her it is no big deal? What happens when a Sweetheart's husband becomes abusive, or when the pastor she goes to for counsel tells her she just needs to be more submissive? What happens when the leader of the women's group she attends starts teaching through a book promoting dangerous advice about disciplining children?

The Sweetheart's problem is that she finds her worth in the acceptance and approval of others, which she earns and maintains through charming compliance. The Sweetheart needs to be taught how to find her inner fighter and advocate appropriately for herself and others, or she will be swept down the path of least resistance.

One of the most effective ways adults can empower adolescent Sweethearts is to pay attention to what we affirm them for. Do we compliment them on their accomplishments, their compliance, their polite behavior and adherence to social expectations? Or do we cheer them on for their courage, their perseverance, and their willingness to tackle hard things, whether they succeed or not? Do we ourselves model a willingness to stretch ourselves and respond to a failed attempt as an opportunity to grow instead of a shameful embarrassment to be avoided at all costs? Congratulate girls for making the team, or getting that part, or winning that scholarship, certainly. But don't forget to compliment the hard work of the girl who didn't make the team, the courage of the girl who stood up for the kid her friends were picking on, and the grit of the girl who struggles in school but keeps working hard, day after day.

It is also important for adults to affirm that it is good and right for Sweethearts to advocate for and defend themselves. Allow them to disagree with you, and talk with them about those disagreements in a calm way that affirms the relationship. Make sure they know that if someone is making them uncomfortable, it is okay to be "rude" and tell the person to stop, walk away, yell, defend themselves, and make a scene. Encourage them to speak up when something is wrong instead of remaining silent for fear of offending someone. Sports, debate, and other competitive extracurriculars may help Sweethearts develop the grit they need to thrive.

Sweethearts don't need to be coddled; they need to be challenged, and they need to be given an extra dose of love, support, and affirmation as they test out their wings.

THE SERVANT

One of the ironies of my work on gender is that I spend most of my time in the company of men. On a recent trip to Kenya, it was not unusual for me to be escorted directly to the living room, to speak with the men as an honored guest, while the women worked in the kitchen, only appearing occasionally with platters of food. Talk about awkward! My timid forays toward the kitchen were met with horrified giggles. I didn't want to scandalize anyone, and I know how self-conscious I would feel if a strange woman was digging around in my kitchen, so for the most part I stayed where I was put. But I still pined for the company of women.

That's why it was such a treat when a group of women let me join their lunch table at a training event in Bondo. They laughed and showed me the proper technique for eating the array of foods on my plate, taught me how to pronounce "thank you" in Luo, and shared what it was like to be a woman in their culture. One of them, a school counselor, launched into a fiery tirade about the challenges dogging her female students. Her primary concern was that girls were expected to spend their evenings cooking, cleaning, and doing household chores while their brothers studied. The girls' schoolwork suffered, and they were often unable to pass the qualifying exams to get into the better schools and universities. This reality affirmed for many adults the belief that girls were not as intelligent as boys and made educating them an even lower priority than it already was. A girl's best chance, the counselor explained, was to be sent to a boarding school where she could focus on her studies and not be bogged down by housework.

Around the world, domestic tasks require an enormous amount of work, and girls are often expected to help their mothers complete them. In rural areas or villages without a well, it is not unusual for girls to spend hours each day fetching water. Sticks and other forms of fuel need to be gathered to keep the fires going. Meals need to be made, clothes need to be laundered, babies need to be tended, and toddlers need to be watched. The larger the family and the fewer modern conveniences they have access to, the less likely the mother is to be able to do it all on her own.

This isn't only an issue in the majority world. When I was doing informal polls on social media, I was surprised at how many women mentioned housework and childcare as significant expectations put on them as teenagers. This isn't all bad, of course. The world would be a happier, healthier place if every boy and girl were equipped with the practical skills needed to run a household. But when a disproportionate amount of adult responsibilities are piled on adolescent girls' shoulders, the developmental work of childhood and the higher education it takes to thrive in the modern world can get pushed aside. For some girls in the Western world, those crushing expectations may look less like housework and more like an unhealthy family obsession with sports, or the performing arts, or perfect grades. Other teens spend their summers and afternoons bringing in income that helps their families. None of these things are wrong in moderation, but burnout is a real danger, and teens need to develop the skills that will help them thrive in adult life. That may or may not involve carrying water five miles a day or executing a perfect pirouette.

Servants are expected to sacrifice their future to the family's immediate need, whether that is a physical need or an emotional need. Globally, one of the best ways to help Servants is by providing easy access to clean water and introducing technology that makes the work traditionally done by women more efficient, allowing them more time for school and self-development. Helping teenage girls build cottage industries that give them more control over their destiny is a good strategy as well. Closer to home, we need to look hard at the expectations we place on teenage girls and ask ourselves: Are those expectations equipping them for adult life, or are they detracting from their development?

THE SIREN

It was a Monday afternoon when the phone rang. One of the pastors from the church I was attending at the time asked if he could drop by to talk about something in person. I agreed, my mind racing as I tossed the wooden train tracks littering the living room into a basket, preparing for his arrival. What could possibly be wrong? Had I written something that offended someone? Had one of my kids misbehaved in the nursery?

As it turns out, an anonymous woman had gone to him with concerns about the blouse I had been wearing on Sunday. She knew I would never *mean* to wear anything provocative, but it was cut low enough that she had seen some cleavage. As my cheeks burned, the pastor assured me that he hadn't seen me on Sunday, so perhaps I should ask my husband what he had thought about the blouse?

I felt crushed, outraged, and utterly humiliated. Besides the embarrassment, this incident introduced an element of insecurity and anxiety into my preparations for church. Were men leering at me as I worshiped? Was I somehow giving the impression that I *wanted* to be leered at? Were my pastors on my side or on the side of the leering men? Were *they* leering men? Was that why they had given the woman's complaint credence? Horrors.

As a young mother in my twenties, I wasn't sure how to deal with this. Now, as a pastor in my forties, I know exactly what to say to anyone coming to me with a complaint about what the young women in our church are wearing: leave those girls alone and get therapy if skinny jeans or spaghetti straps send you into paroxysms of lust.

Certainly, modesty is important—more about that later. But it is also subjective, and not nearly as important as young women in church feeling safe, secure, and valued for something besides their bodies.

People have been placing the blame for sexual temptation and even sexual assault on the shoulders of young women since time immemorial. Certainly, most adolescents (and adults) want to feel attractive. But our collective obsession with young female bodies creates a dynamic in which women's bodies are treated like sexual objects to be either shown off or covered up, instead of the functional, God-given gift that they are. The results are not pretty. Eating disorders, self-esteem problems, and sexual issues abound, sometimes in girls who haven't even reached puberty yet. Some girls sexualize themselves in a desperate bid for love and acceptance, trying to be whatever those around them want them to be. Some take refuge under baggy clothes, extra pounds, dark makeup, or forbidding attitudes.

The Siren is the girl who receives so many messages about her physicality that her other attributes are overshadowed. She may be particularly shapely, or attractive, or an early bloomer, or she may simply live in a sex-obsessed context. In any case, Sirens are forced to live under the weight and expectations of other people's sexuality, whether that sexuality manifests as lascivious behavior or prudish control. They desperately need that weight to be lifted so they can find their value and identity in God, not in what other people think about their bodies.

Compliment Sirens on things other than their looks; brag up their character, their intelligence, their hard work, their sense of humor. Pay attention to the images of women you are exposed to and take an inventory about how those images influence your—and their—perspective. Help Sirens rediscover their bodies as strong, useful things that can throw balls, cook and consume meals, rake a neighbor's leaves, and hug a hurting friend. And be willing to function as a shield, sheltering them from inappropriate sexual attention, even the kind that comes from the modesty police. Teach them to be wise and to honor God with their choices, of course, but don't expect them to carry the weight of other people's sin.

TWO

Getting Schooled

GIRLS AND EDUCATION

Consoler collapsed to the curb at the bus stop, acrid fumes from the passing traffic stinging her lungs as she gasped for breath. Her back ached from the beating she had just escaped, and the sun pounded mercilessly on her head, but it all paled in comparison to the pain in her heart.

It had all been for nothing. The miles she had walked for the two hours of classes she could fit in while her young cousin was at school. How angry she had made Auntie when she said she didn't want to marry the newspaper salesman—even though he himself didn't want to marry a girl too young to have breasts—and the abuse that had led to. The ridicule she had endured, showing up to school unwashed, unwanted, and unloved. She had fought for every number, letter, and word she had learned, but it didn't make any difference now.

Consoler had gone to school that morning hoping they would let her take the test she needed to qualify for secondary school, even though Auntie refused to pay her school fees. Her teacher had not only refused but had berated and beaten her for having the gall to show up without money.

Tears blurred Consoler's eyes as she yanked her composition book out of her satchel, staring at all the wasted work. But a gentle, insistent voice inside her head refused to let her lose hope. She remembered how her uncle told her God would help her someday, and she couldn't get the thought out of her mind. She wiped her eyes with the corner of her filthy sleeve, grabbed her pencil, and began writing the letter that would change her life: "Dear God, if you only let me get through high school, I will spend the rest of my life helping girls like me."

As Consoler poured her pain out to God, a whole new future began to take shape in her mind. What she needed was a mama who would love her and take care of her, just like her grandma used to, before she died. Well, she would become the mama she herself needed. She would find girls who needed help and give them a bed to sleep in and good food to eat. They would not have to sleep sitting up in a closet or eat scraps from the garbage. She would buy them underwear so they could keep themselves clean during their periods, and she would get money for their school fees so they wouldn't have to worry about their future. And she would never, ever, ever hit them, even if they were bad. Never. But first, with God's help, she needed to find *some* way to finish her education.

An idea winged its way into Consoler's head, and suddenly she knew what to do. It didn't matter if people made fun of her. It didn't matter if people mistook her for a prostitute. It didn't matter if people chased her, or scolded her, or told her no. She was going to finish school, one way or another.

She stashed her composition book in her satchel, picked herself up off the ground, and headed downtown to beg for school fees.

FEMALE EDUCATION AND INTERNATIONAL DEVELOPMENT

Consoler is a remarkable woman who grew up to do exactly what she promised. She not only qualified for and graduated from high school; she got a scholarship to college, used her aid money to help pay other girls' school fees, and moved a couple of particularly desperate young women off the street into her dorm room. She founded New Hope for Girls in Dar es Salaam, Tanzania, and works with local schools to identify and intervene on behalf of girls who are being abused. When the situation is particularly desperate, Consoler still brings them home with her, although instead of a cramped dorm room, now it is to the complex she shares with her husband and two biological children. The last time I was in Tanzania, there were twenty-eight girls living with Consoler, and each one called her Mama. Mama, Consoler: never have two names been so well earned.

Given Consoler's heart, I have no doubt that she would have found some way to help others, with or without an education. But her effectiveness would have been hindered, and she knew it. Even as a young teen, Consoler instinctively understood what development experts have been trumpeting for years: educating women is not only the most effective way to move them from risk to resilience but is the most effective way to transform the entire community.

The statistics are startling. Growing up, I certainly didn't associate high school with personal safety or the greater social good. But study after study has shown that high school, against all odds, may be the most transformative social institution in the world.

First there is the economic benefit. Every year of primary school that a girl attends increases her earning potential by 10 to 20 percent, and each year of secondary school increases it by 15 to 25 percent.[1] That is an astonishing return on investment—a return that reaps dividends over the course of a woman's lifetime, not just for her but for her entire family system. It is often the woman's income that breaks the cycle of extreme poverty; in part because two incomes are better than one, but mainly because women tend to allocate their money differently than men. While men only reinvest 30–40 percent of their income into their families, women pour 90 percent of their earnings right back into their children, making sure they have the food, shelter, healthcare, and education they need to thrive.[2]

During a recent trip to Uganda, I was surprised to discover that many married couples kept their finances strictly separate, and that older women often advised younger women to buy a plot of land and keep it secret from their husband. They could retreat to it with their children if their husband became impossible to live with, or if he died and his family tried to reclaim his land. But they could also use it as a source of income, renting it out to tenants or even using it to grow crops themselves. My first reaction was shock at the idea of a married couple hiding assets from one another; my second was admiration for the women who did what they needed to do to safeguard their children's future, despite any shenanigans their partner or his family might try to pull.

Girls who attend school also marry later and have fewer children, both important factors for health, safety, and economic security. In 2018, UNICEF published a series of surveys looking at the state of child unions around the world. At the time of writing, 11 percent of girls between the ages of fifteen and nineteen in Latin America and the Caribbean are married or living in a domestic partnership. Those numbers rise to 13 percent in the Middle East and North Africa, 19 percent in South Asia, and 20–24 percent across the rest of Africa. Globally, about one in six adolescent girls is married or in a domestic partnership.[3]

As shocking as those numbers are, they actually represent significant progress made in an astonishingly short time. The same study shows that young women currently between the ages of twenty and twenty-four were significantly more likely to have been married or in a domestic partnership before their eighteenth birthday, to the tune of 40 percent across Africa, 30 percent in South Asia, and 17 percent in the Middle East and North Africa.[4] It is unsurprising that much of this progress came hand in hand with sweeping educational initiatives and a push to abolish school fees.

Marrying or partnering off at such a young age makes girls vulnerable to a variety of problems that will be addressed later in this book, and is considered by many to be a violation of basic human rights. However, education is one of the best safeguards against early marriage. Statistically, even seven years of education means that a young woman growing up in the majority world will marry four years later and have 2.2 fewer children than those with no education.[5]

And children of educated mothers typically fare better, whether they're growing up in Nebraska or Namibia. It's

not just about economics; the information, critical thinking skills, and social networks women acquire in school are
pressed into service for their children. Sometimes it is a matter of survival. A thirty-one-year-old mother with a tenth-
grade education has a different set of skills to draw on when
she suspects something is not quite right with her baby than
that of a thirteen-year-old mother who never learned how to
read. Sometimes it's a matter of development. A widely touted
2003 article titled "The Early Catastrophe: The 30 Million
Word Gap by Age 3" explained that in the United States,
children from professional (and highly educated) families
heard 2,153 words per waking hour, kids from working class
homes heard 1,251 words per hour, and children growing up
in poverty heard only 616 words per hour. This translated
into differences in vocabulary development that affected later
academic achievement.[6] Sometimes it's simply a matter of a
mother's advantages being passed directly to her children.
When a woman makes decent money, she can cover her children's school fees. When a woman understands algebra, she
can help her children with their homework. When a woman
has made it to university, she is better able to help her children navigate the admissions process themselves. The more
resources a mother has at her disposal, the more her children
do too, and education is the most valuable resource of all.

Perhaps the most startling statistic about the benefits of
secondary education is related to disease prevention. It is estimated that worldwide, six thousand people are newly infected with HIV every day. Two-thirds of those people are
young women living in sub-Saharan Africa. In fact, females
between the ages of fifteen and twenty-four are *eight times*
more likely to be infected with HIV/AIDS than their male

peers.[7] Some of this can be attributed to sexual violence, but most of it stems from young women being partnered off with older men who have had multiple sexual partners. A young woman may be married off for dowry money, or move in with a man to escape a miserable home life, or find a "sugar daddy" who will bankroll her education in exchange for sex on demand. A friend who lives in Nairobi told me of the cars that line up outside the universities on Friday nights, filled with married men waiting to pick up that evening's entertainment. It sounds far-fetched, but the stories I've heard from other women suggest that this is one of those situations where truth is stranger than fiction. There is hope, though. Predatory sugar daddies aside, young women enrolled in secondary school are five times less likely to be infected with HIV than those who are not in school.[8]

It doesn't take a degree in international development to see the pattern here. Teenage girls need to be in school, for their own good, and for the good of the world.

WILY WOLVES, DECEIVED SHEPHERDESSES, AND THE SCANDAL OF FEMALE EDUCATION, RELIGIOUS AND OTHERWISE

One of the most frequently employed "clobber passages" used to silence women and restrict them from positions of authority is 1 Timothy 2:11-14: "A woman should learn in quietness and full submission. I do not permit a woman to teach or to assume authority over a man; she must be quiet. For Adam was formed first, then Eve. And Adam was not the one deceived; it was the woman who was deceived and became a sinner."

This seems a bit odd coming from a man who often referred to women as co-laborers and fellow ministers. People have been debating what the apostle Paul meant in these instructions to Timothy for a long time, and are unlikely to stop anytime soon. As a female pastor who takes biblical authority very seriously, I agree that it is an important discussion to stay engaged in. One of the great ironies about the modern debate on this topic, though, is that we get so focused on Paul's insistence on quietness and submission that we miss the revolutionary word which kicked off the whole affair.

Learn.

A woman should *learn*.

There is a story in the Talmud about a wise and wealthy woman who asked Rabbi Eliezer, a first-century rabbi just a generation after Paul, a question about the events in Exodus. He responded by telling her that there was no wisdom in a woman apart from her skill with a spindle, and that she had no business asking theological questions—even if the rest of his students were waiting with bated breath to hear how he would answer her fascinating query. When Rabbi Eliezer's son, who was present at the time, asked him why he couldn't have just answered the woman's question instead of offending a big donor, he said that it would be better for the Torah to be burned than to be taught to a woman.[9]

Some wealthy Roman women were graced with an education, and Jewish women were taught what they needed to know to be good kosher housewives. But women in the ancient world were not typically educated, and they certainly did not receive a theological education. In fact, many scholars believe that the problems Paul was addressing in 1 Timothy had to do with uneducated young widows, who suddenly had access to a dizzying array of knowledge that had been closed off to them before. Christians had flung the door to female education wide open, but false teachers were taking advantage of the situation, going from house to house (or perhaps house church to house church) undermining the apostles' teaching and encouraging their new protégées to do the same. Widows were particularly vulnerable, without a more educated counterpart to ask crucial questions, and there is some insinuation that the motives of the male false teachers may not have been entirely religious. Paul was clear on what needed to happen: the offending men were to be kicked out, but the women, who were victims of their scam and didn't know any better, simply needed to stop parroting the heretical nonsense they had been fed and be instructed in the truth. They certainly could not aspire to positions involving teaching or leading while they were steeped in deception. They needed to quiet their hearts, minds, and voices—and they needed to learn.

It is hard to fathom how radical Christianity seemed in those first few centuries, particularly in the worth, dignity, and freedom it afforded women. It is hard for contemporary readers—who grew up on stories of Jesus in a world he had already turned upside down—to fathom how radical he was. Rabbi Eliezer answered women's questions with insults and obstruction. Rabbi Jesus, on the other hand, taught women, traveled with women, healed women, defended women, told parables about women, and appointed a woman, who couldn't even testify in court, to be the first witness to his resurrection. The longest conversation Jesus had with anyone in the Gospels was a deeply theological conversation with a Samaritan woman who was living with a man she wasn't married to. Even his disciples were scandalized by that one! Dorothy Sayers writes in *Are Women Human?*:

Perhaps it is no wonder that the women were first at the Cradle and last at the Cross. They had never known a man like this Man—there never has been such another. A prophet and teacher who never nagged at them, never flattered or coaxed or patronized; who never made arch jokes about them, never treated them either as "The women, God help us!" or "The ladies, God bless them"; who rebuked without querulousness and praised without condescension; who took their questions and arguments seriously. . . . There is no act, no sermon, no parable in the whole Gospel that borrows its pungency from female perversity; nobody could possibly guess from the words and deeds of Jesus that there was anything "funny" about woman's nature.[10]

Preach it, Sister Dorothy!

MARY, MARY, QUITE CONTRARY

Mary of Bethany is one of my favorite characters in the Bible. She is like the Anne of Green Gables of the New Testament, forever scandalizing onlookers with her conspicuous lack of impulse control. Think about it. Can you think of even one story involving Mary of Bethany that didn't have the Pharisees, the disciples, or even her own sister clutching their metaphorical pearls? The tears. The hair. The perfume. The sheer, unseemly drama of it all. The only time raised eyebrows weren't explicitly mentioned was that time she flung herself at Jesus and scolded him for not showing up soon enough to save her brother, and well, I suspect eyebrows were raised. Jesus himself broke down and bawled. And yet Jesus always stuck up for her.

The most famous story about Mary of Bethany, of course, is the tiff she got into with her sister Martha—or rather, the tiff Martha got into with *her*. Jesus and his entourage had shown up at their house in Bethany, and Martha was playing the good Jewish hostess, knocking herself out trying to get them all fed while Mary sat at Jesus' feet. Finally, Martha lost her temper and insisted that Jesus tell Mary to help her in the kitchen. Jesus spoke kindly to Martha but took Mary's side, insisting that she had chosen the better thing, and it would not be taken from her (Luke 10:38-42).

It's always interesting to listen to how people teach this story. Sometimes a man stands behind a pulpit and pontificates about how spending time with God is more important than everything else—while his wife is home taking care of sick kids, and the women of the church are minding the nursery, teaching junior church, and setting up for the potluck he'll attend after the service. Sometimes a Bible study leader jumps to Martha's defense, pointing out that Jesus wasn't *scolding* her, but just saying that Mary's way was *better*. And Jesus *did* want to eat, didn't he? Sometimes, Mary is portrayed as a contemplative, introspective woman, which always makes me giggle. Contemplative and introspective, sure—but in a very aggressive sort of way!

Here's what most of us miss. Martha wasn't just worried and upset because she had a big meal to put on. She was, in all likelihood, worried and upset because her scandalous baby sister was "sitting at Jesus' feet." That didn't mean Mary was doing her best imitation of a housecat. It meant she had positioned herself as a disciple—something only men were supposed to do in that culture. Remember Rabbi Eliezer, telling the wise woman to get back to her spindle and thread? Martha was telling Jesus to tell Mary to get back to the kitchen. But Jesus not only defended Mary's right to sit at his feet; he said that it was the best possible place for her to be.

To this day, when I hear about seminaries that won't allow women to register for certain courses or enroll in certain degree programs, I think about Jesus' words to Martha: "Mary has chosen what is better, and it will not be taken away from her" (Luke 10:42).

Are you listening, church?

Are you really, really listening to Jesus' extraordinary, earth-shattering, extremely good news?

FAMILY, FAITH, AND FLOUTING TRADITION: A PERSONAL REFLECTION

I'm a college dropout. In fact, I dropped out of college twice before finally settling in and finishing my bachelor's degree in my mid-thirties, when I was married with four kids, and then going on to seminary. It's not that I didn't want to go to college. I did. It's not that my family didn't support my endeavors—my parents had been paying my way through college when I dropped out the first time, and my husband has never been anything but supportive.

It's just that college wasn't really something women in my family *did*. Even my brilliant aunt, who was valedictorian of her high school class and could have gotten a free ride to the engineering school of her choice, dropped out of the local college before the first semester was up. The women in my family had the brains to excel, but we lacked the imagination to see what academically excellent women could become. So many of us lost heart and defaulted to the path we knew—the path that led right back into the kitchen. Maybe, deep down inside, that's the path we thought we belonged on anyway, the only path that was truly open to virtuous Christian women.

Some values are caught, not taught.

In fairness to my female relatives, college wasn't really something *anyone* in my family did until my father's generation—and precious few of the men finished either. I'm always astonished when people talk about grandparents who went to college. Only two of my grandparents finished high school, and that was by the skin of their teeth. We're descended from "dirt scratchers," as my father called them: desperately poor subsistence farmers from the backwoods of Ontario, the grasslands of Missouri, and the craggy Kentucky hills. They crisscrossed the continent in covered wagons pulled by mules, searching for land, and work, and anything they could find to keep body and soul together. There were a few scrappy immigrants thrown in for good measure—a Polish man who fled the German conquest of his homeland to work as a farmhand in North Dakota, and a Norwegian woman who crossed the Atlantic to serve as a maid in an iron baron's mansion.

My ancestors were whip sharp, but education wasn't exactly a priority for them. Survival was. Throw your body down on the altar of hard labor, hoe until your shoulders seize, and scrub your fingers right down to the bone—and maybe your children could have a better life than you. That was their way. Who could afford education when there was so much work to be done right now?

It was writing that scared me into going back to college. One of my first articles—a rather snarky, satirical piece taking aim at religious legalism—had been accepted for publication in a magazine I had found listed in *Writer's Digest*. I did a happy dance, cashed the check they sent me . . . and only then found out how high the circulation of the magazine was. I almost choked on my celebratory cheesecake.

Apparently, I was one of about five people in the English-speaking world who had never heard of this magazine before stumbling across their submission guidelines. It rattled me, thinking of my words going out to all those people—more people than my pastor, with all his careful study and advanced degrees, would ever speak to in his lifetime. I didn't think I had written anything off base, but what if I had? And had I written it in the right way—in a way that would build up the body of Christ and make us all better? Or had I just profited off a cheap shot to a certain segment of the church that resonated with disgruntled survivors?

I wasn't sure. But I decided then and there that if my words were going to reach a broader audience than my pastor's, I had better have at least as much education as he did. My hunger for knowledge was beginning to reach a fever pitch as well. I was an intelligent woman who had been studying the Bible for years, but I wanted a theological underpinning I just wasn't getting from Beth Moore studies, commentaries rescued from the free bin at the library, and the few precious books I had splurged on at an InterVarsity Bible and Life conference. God had given me a voice. Now I needed to find someone's feet to sit at and learn how to use that voice faithfully.

I am eternally grateful for the people who helped me along the way—Marcia Jamison, Gaylan Mathiesen, and especially my pastor Darrell Nelson, who mentored me through three years of undergraduate education (including helping me with Greek and Hebrew!) and then spurred me on to go to seminary when the cost and commitment seemed overwhelming. Other encouragers? Roger and Mary Risley, who after hearing that I was considering seminary, gave me a fifty-dollar check wrapped in a note that said "The Risley Fund for Women in Seminary." It covered my admission fee. My grandma IrmaDel—the one who had never finished high school—would occasionally show up at my door with fresh-baked buns and rhubarb upside-down cake and fold laundry while I did homework. The women of the Redbud Writers Guild, who showed me what women could do with a theological education.

I was an intelligent American woman with all the privileges inherent in that, yet it took a small army to get me through school. Some days the demands of work and family on top of finishing seminary still make me feel as if I am facing down a giant with only a slingshot, because some kid ran off with my rocks.

Perhaps all this is why I sympathize with the Ephesian women Paul was talking about in 1 Timothy: natural leaders and would-be teachers who were eager to learn, and learn well, if only given the chance. Perhaps this is why I sympathize with their modern-day descendants as well: rogue female Bible teachers who can't help but lead, but occasionally end up leading people astray.

NEGLECTED PROPHETESSES AND SELF-FULFILLING PROPHECIES

The book was lying on a side table in my mother's library. It didn't look like her usual fare, so I picked it up and flipped through the first few pages, curious. Before I knew it, I was drawn in, watching in horrified fascination as the chapters unfolded. The author combined her strong opinions about how Christian families were supposed to run with personal anecdotes, proof texts wrenched from their biblical context, and dangerous advice that could, very easily, lead to women dying. Women were not only encouraged to forgo any form of contraception, and men to have surgery to reverse their vasectomies; couples were admonished to continue pursuing pregnancy against medical advice. There was at least one story of a terminally ill woman who had been cured by becoming pregnant. The goal was to have as many children as possible—a quiverful of children raised in a patriarchal, ultraconservative environment—and the outcome was in God's hands.

"Where did you get this?" I asked my mother, aghast, when she had returned from her errands. She rolled her eyes and told me that one of the women from the church we were both attending at the time had put it in her mailbox.

I frowned. The woman she named was part of a group within the church who tended to homeschool their children, wear long dresses, birth their babies at home, and prefer old-fashioned ways to contemporary ones. It wasn't an impermeable group—several of those women were dear friends and mentors—and the line between crunchy earth mama and ultraconservative Quiverfull adherent wasn't always clear. Recently, however, some of them had taken to wearing head coverings, and I had heard rumors that one of them was starting to promote the doctrine of sinless perfection to the younger women in the church. Goodness knows I had no problem with hats. But I had a big problem with heresy, and with teachings that put women in danger.

This was the third time in as many months that I had heard about these women aggressively targeting other women whom they wanted to influence with their views, right under the nose of the church leadership. Did the pastors have *any* idea what these women were reading, and pressing on other congregants impressed by their ascetic lifestyle? The short answer is that they did not—at least, not until the situation blew up in their faces, resulting in relational and spiritual scars that linger to this day. But they should have. If they had paid more attention to the education of the women in the church—if they had expressed more interest in what the women were reading, and teaching, and talking about and in what was happening in the official and unofficial women's Bible studies—those problems could have been headed off at the pass.

What made the situation even more tragic is that many of the women involved were natural-born leaders who meant nothing but good. They were simply starving for spiritual knowledge they probably would have gotten if they had been born male, and they filled those gaps in the best way they knew. Consider their lives. Homeschooling kept their minds sharp and active. Asceticism provided a rigorous challenge the church was certainly not offering them. They devoured books, magazines, and publications put out by their favorite ministries—although unfortunately, those materials were often self-published by small "ministries" run by individuals and families, with no vetting or accountability to larger structures and often no formal education to back it up.

They were starving, and they found people who took them seriously enough to feed them something substantial. They were just being fed the wrong things—and feeding others the wrong things in turn.

I can't help but wonder how differently things might have gone if some of those women could have conceived of a career in ministry when they were younger and gotten training toward that end. If the Bible studies they attended had focused less on the Proverbs 31 woman and more on Jesus. If, when they expressed concern about non–King James translations of the Bible, someone would have helped them learn the original languages so they could study them for themselves. What might these women have become if a wise mentor had come alongside them and offered them the real spiritual meat they so desperately craved?

And it almost certainly would have had to be a male mentor at that time. Because before I determined to become for others what I had lacked—a pastor who was a woman—there were no women in our seven-hundred-member church who had formal theological training. And until I virtually kicked down the doors of the lead pastor's office with a copy of my recent publications in hand, insisting that I needed help and he was the only one qualified for the job, that would have been nearly unthinkable. It just wasn't done.

And therein lies the problem with women's education, in the church and around the world. It's a classic case of "Whoever has will be given more, and they will have an abundance. Whoever does not have, even what they have will be taken from them" (Matthew 25:29). Women appear to prove their ignorance because they lack access to knowledge traditionally reserved for men. Time and again, this is touted as proof of women's unsuitability to access knowledge traditionally reserved for men.

Church, we've got to get the girls to school. And women, the first step in getting the girls to school might be getting yourself back to school as well. Some of us need to blaze the trail for the younger women coming behind us and become the pastors, teachers, and mentors we lacked in the process. If you won't do it for yourself, do it for the girls.

CRUSHING BARRIERS TO GIRLS' EDUCATION

I was sitting at a table at an outdoor café, trying unsuccessfully to keep my waffle cone from dissolving as some friends I had just run into grilled me about the book I was working on. When I brought up girls' education, one of them sighed.

"Here, the biggest barrier to girls learning is the other girls," she said, as I swiped her napkin and mopped raspberry ice cream off my palm. "You remember I used to teach middle school, right? Kids can be so cruel at that age." She went on to talk about bullying, queen bees, and how female participation dropped when just one boy was introduced into the classroom. This was on top of all the other things happening to them during the tumultuous early teen years. My friend would have her students start each day by journaling, watch their faces as they wrote, and check in with anyone who seemed to be upset or in distress. "It seemed like every day, I had a girl starting her period for the first time, or dealing with a crisis at home, but sometimes, they just felt humiliated because there was something wrong with the zipper on their coat, and their mom made them wear it anyway."

It's the same in other parts of the world. One woman told me about how excited she had been when the woman who came through their village selling secondhand shoes let her have a leftover pair for free. At least, she was excited until she went to school the next day, and the other kids pointed out that the shoes didn't exactly match. "I ran to the toilet and sobbed," she said, echoing a nearly universal experience among preteen girls. "It's one thing to go to school barefoot, but when you show up with shoes that don't match?" She shook her head sadly. "I threw them down the pit and ran home."

Oh, sweet girls. It's not easy being young and female.

My friend was right. Even when adolescent girls have access to a good educational system, plenty of barriers prevent them from reaching their potential. Interestingly, the issues she brought up are not unrelated to the problems that keep young women out of school entirely in other parts of the world—not having a way to manage their periods, not having access to the right sort of clothing, family problems that infringe on their education, and general harassment.

So what are the barriers that interfere with young women getting the education they need? And how can we help knock them down?

UNDERFUNDED SCHOOLS AND OUT-OF-REACH SCHOOL FEES

"That was my wife," Roger said, setting his phone down on the passenger seat. "I need to pick my son up from school. Do you mind if I get him before I drop you off? It is on the way to the hotel."

My husband and I readily agreed. Roger had been a gracious host, explaining all sorts of fascinating details about Entebbe as he drove us around his home city, and now he struck up a conversation about schools: where he had gone to school, where his daughter went to school, and why he and his wife had chosen a Montessori school for their son. When we got to the topic of free, government-run schools in Uganda, he shook his head.

"It is very hard. The teachers—sometimes they will go months without being paid. So if you are not being paid, and your child is sick, or you need to buy food—what would you do? There are schools, but there are not always teachers. Most people, if they can afford it, send their children to private school."

Free primary schools are becoming more common across Africa, and Uganda was the first country in sub-Saharan Africa to introduce free, universal secondary education, back in 2007.[11] Several others followed suit. Enrollment skyrocketed, and great strides have been made, especially for girls and students from impoverished households. However, households still bear a disproportionate amount of the cost of educating their children, and the infrastructure has not caught up with the need.

It's one thing to guarantee students an education. It's another thing to actually provide it.

This is not only the case in low-income countries. In her story "The Problem We All Live With" on the radio show *This American Life*, Nikole Hannah-Jones chronicles the situation of a school district in Missouri, just outside Saint Louis. "Here's how the Normandy School District was performing," she says. "Points for academic achievement in English—zero, math—zero, social studies—zero, science—zero, points for college placement—zero. It seems impossible, but in eleven of thirteen measures, the district didn't earn a single point. Ten out of 140 points, that was its score. . . . It's like they got ten points just for existing."[12]

When my parents moved to Kansas City a couple of years back, they were quickly made aware of a belief so ingrained it could have been gospel: if you have school-age kids, you *have* to live on the Kansas side. Otherwise, you need to send your kids to private school.

My initial shock—that anyone would say something so racist, elitist, and alarmist—was eclipsed only by the shock I felt when I learned more about the state of public education in Missouri. There was definitely cause for alarm. Living in the upper Midwest, I had never heard of a public school district being stripped of its accreditation. I didn't even know that could happen! How was it possible, in America, for children to be sent to schools that were failing so badly that the board of education gave them a big ole F? Given the option, I wouldn't want to send my kids to a failing school either. But what about parents and kids who *don't* have an option?

Education is a good investment. Study after study has shown that money poured into education comes back in increased earning potential, which means a wealthier populace and more tax dollars for the government. In the United States, the wage gap between college and high school graduates has reached an all-time high, with college graduates earning an astonishing 56 percent more than high school grads in 2015 and gobbling up most of the new jobs. The number of employed college graduates has gone up 21 percent since the Great Recession, while the number of employed high school graduates has dropped by 8 percent.[13] The numbers—and the dollar signs—speak for themselves.

Yet education is also cultural and political. One would think, given the obvious economic benefits of university education, that Americans would be anxious to crank more people through the system. However, there is resistance to the idea of making college tuition-free, largely rooted in anxieties about the cost to taxpayers and a general sense that students should work for a college education, not just academically but financially. Certainly, making college tuition-free would cost money. But what is it costing Americans, on the human, social, and economic level, to *not* provide free college education?

Helping young people achieve their potential should not be a political issue. It is a no-brainer that should unite people from every walk of life, all around the world. However, education requires an upfront investment of human and economic capital for dividends that will not be realized for many years—whether it is a government picking up the cost of educating its youth or parents choosing to send their daughters to school instead of keeping them home to work or marrying them off for dowry money. It also requires smart policy making and a steely commitment to doing what it takes to make things better for *all* young people.

Globally, we can invest in the future by offering to pick up the tab for tuition, collectively and individually. This is not as expensive as one might think. In fact, the estimated cost of providing an education to every child in the world is less than American women spend on cosmetics every year.[14] The question is not whether we have the money; it is whether we have the moral will. Many nations are simply unable to cover the cost of educating their youth, however much they might want to. They need international aid to make that happen. Many families are simply unable to cover the cost of educating their children, however much they might want to. There are hundreds if not thousands of nonprofits that offer people the opportunity to sponsor a child's education or support a school. Through a lending organization like Kiva, you can make a microfinance loan to a "mom-preneur" struggling to put her kids through school.

Locally, we can begin by finding out what the state of education is in our own communities. What struggles do our students, teachers, and schools face, and how can we best support them? Are there schools in our area that are doing much better or much worse than neighboring schools? If so, why? And what should we as followers of Jesus do about it—other than enrolling our children in the better schools?

I am not an educator, and I do not know the answer to all these questions. But I do know that a lot is riding on people's willingness to educate themselves about the importance of education and to allocate their resources accordingly.

MENSTRUATION

Taboos surrounding menstruation have been around from time immemorial. In fairness to the ancients, it had to be disconcerting: bleeding is usually associated with an injury, with death and guilt and tragedy. Was there something wrong with women, inside, that made them bleed every month? Myths sprang up to explain this strange phenomenon, and cultures around the world, feeling that it was better to be safe than sorry, imposed restrictions on menstruating women that made sense to them. Leviticus decrees that "when a woman has her regular flow of blood, the impurity of her monthly period will last seven days, and anyone who touches her will be unclean till evening. . . . Anyone who touches anything she sits on will be unclean; they must wash their clothes and bathe with water, and they will be unclean till evening" (Leviticus 15:19, 22).

Stay out of the kitchen. Stay out of the temple. Stay away from the men. I've heard many women joke that some of those restrictions don't sound half bad. But for millions of girls around the world, the stigma attached to menstruation is anything but funny.

In an article about period-shaming for *Self* magazine, Puja Changoiwala describes what happened when a classmate in Mumbai noticed blood from her first period spotting her uniform: her friends circled around her and whisked her to the teacher, who discreetly slipped a sanitary pad into her pocket.[15] She was one of the lucky ones. Girls in India miss an average of six days of school per month because of their periods, and 23 percent drop out of school altogether once they hit puberty.[16] In Kenya, only about half of adolescent girls have access to sanitary pads.[17] Women have told me about using rags and plant fibers to catch their flow, or even soil or ash wrapped in fabric or an old sock. Even these ineffective and unhygienic forms of period management depend on having undergarments that can hold them in place, and many girls don't.

Even when girls do have access to sanitary pads, schools often lack the washroom facilities girls need to manage their periods in a hygienic, culturally sensitive way. Is there water near the toilet to clean up with, or do you have to go to a public area? Is there a place to dispose of used pads discreetly, or would you be dropping them into the same pit toilet the boys use? Some girls go home to change their sanitary pads, but obviously that isn't an option for everyone. Some girls try to make it through the whole day without changing whatever they are using to manage their period, putting them at risk for infection.

Finances aren't the primary problem here. Sanitary pads are cheap. (Although even in the Western world, the "pink tax" makes them far more expensive than they should be. Why are items made for women more expensive than comparable items made for men? And why are many places still taxing feminine hygiene products as if they were a luxury item instead of a basic necessity? Not cool.) No, the primary problem stems from social taboos, making girls too embarrassed to go to school for fear blood might leak onto their clothing; making it difficult for women to find and buy feminine hygiene products, particularly in rural areas; making girls reticent to leave used sanitary pads in a toilet shared with boys; making it difficult to have frank conversations about why teenage girls are missing so much school and how to best address it.

Happily, many people are beginning to defy and dismantle social taboos, normalizing conversations about menstruation and making it easier for girls to access the supplies they need to manage their periods. Structural changes, particularly surrounding school toilet facilities, are needed. Still, because sanitary pads are small and inexpensive, it's relatively easy for individuals and organizations to make a big dent in this problem, once they become aware of its politely veiled existence.

Social enterprises such as Afripads and Aakar Innovations not only produce problem-solving menstrual supplies; they provide jobs for women, effectively raising awareness and promoting period management as a social good. Quick-drying, reusable Afripads come with a discreet storage bag and are made at a workshop in rural Uganda. Aakar's compostable, inexpensive Anandi pads are made from locally sourced materials in female-run mini factories around the world. Newer solutions, such as period panties and menstrual cups, remain out of reach in many parts of the world because of economic or cultural concerns. But many of the businesses selling those products donate part of their profits to organizations providing menstrual supplies to schoolgirls.

Days for Girls is a great organization that distributes cleverly camouflaged PODS (portable objects of dignity), including pretty, waterproof shields made of dark print fabrics and absorbent liners that look like washcloths. This means that after washing them, women can hang them out to dry without embarrassment, instead of stashing them away in a hidden place, putting the fabric at risk for mildew. Days for Girls provides several ways for concerned individuals to get involved, from supporting women who make PODS in their local communities as a social enterprise to joining a Days for Girls chapter in your area and sewing and assembling menstrual kits yourself. Or simply send seven dollars per month—about what American women spend on menstrual supplies—to the charity of your choosing.

Oh, and while you're at it? Don't forget to add a box of tampons the next time you drop donations off at your local food bank or women's shelter.

WOMEN'S WORK

Some girls are out of school because their families can't afford the tuition. Some are out of school because their families can't afford the supplies they need. And many, many adolescent girls are out of school because their families can't afford to lose their labor around the house, on the farm, at the market, or in the factory.

Even when girls are enrolled in school, domestic duties often infringe on their studies in a way that would be unthinkable for their brothers. "You will see children coming home from school," my friend Alan told me, explaining the situation in western Kenya. "The boys are playing, and the girls are picking up sticks for the fire. In the evening, boys are studying while their sisters are cooking supper, washing, doing everything. Then girls don't do as well on the exams, and people say, 'See? Girls aren't as well suited to education.'"

This book is about how a strategic focus on adolescent girls helps women, children, and all of society. But when it comes to this issue of traditionally female work, in the home or in the marketplace, we need to swap out our lens and look at how helping women helps adolescent girls. Women have a lot on their plate. Around the world, women make up about 40 percent of the workforce.[18] They also do the lion's share of unpaid domestic work—twice as much as men in the industrial world, and three times as much in the majority world.[19] Traditional female work is particularly time consuming in rural areas and in families that don't have access to modern appliances. There is fuel to be gathered, water to be fetched, meals to be cooked (often from scratch and over a fire), and clothes to be washed and mended by hand. If the family is fortunate enough to have a garden or a small farm, the women often manage that too. By the time there is an adolescent girl in the mix, it is a safe bet that there are other children in the family as well—siblings who require more food, clothing, and social resources if they are older, and more oversight and direct care if they are younger. It is one thing for a young mother to strap a baby onto her back and do the work needed to sustain three people. It is another thing for a mother to manage it all by herself with five children underfoot while also working outside the home.

I mean, I have a washer, a dryer, a microwave, and a supportive husband, and I still succumb to Sisyphean domestic despair at least once every two weeks. Sometimes, the task seems impossible. Sometimes, the task truly *is* impossible.

And when mothers need help in cultures where males dissociate themselves from traditionally female work, it tends to fall on the shoulders of young teenage girls—either the mothers' own daughters or someone else's daughter who has been sent to live with and work for them, a common arrangement in many parts of the world. Young women in this second group are particularly vulnerable, especially when resources are scarce or when the girl or her mother is viewed as competition for the woman or children the girl is living with.

It is not that many women wouldn't prefer for their daughters to be in school. It is that they honestly cannot make it without their daughter helping with childcare or domestic chores or bringing in supplementary income. So how can we help women help their daughters?

Helping women gain easy access to clean water for cooking, washing, and drinking is a great start. It is not unusual for school-age girls to walk miles every day to get water. Supporting well or water collection projects is a simple way to cut down on this, providing precious hours that girls can spend in school instead of hauling water. Access to clean water also means that children are less likely to get sick and miss school. Just one aside: many Western water projects include men perceived to be the local leaders but neglect to include women in the decision-making, building, and maintenance process. This is a critical error, since women are typically the ones responsible for water collection and are much more invested in making sure it works. Try to support water projects that include women's insights and teach them how to maintain the water source. If you already support a water project that does not do this, suggest that they consider expanding women's roles in their projects.

Direct financial support through child sponsorship or microfinance loans to mothers can be a big help, as mentioned earlier. But it would also help women and girls if we became more aware of the industries in which females tend to work and the impact our buying decisions have on them. The clothing industry comes to mind. If you have a moment, go to your closet and pull out a pair of jeans. Where were they made? Who laid the fabric out, cut it, and stitched it together with fleet fingers? Turn the pockets inside out and take a good look at them. Did you know each one was stitched separately and added by hand?

As easy as it is for us to forget when we purchase our clothing in generic, brightly lit stores, our clothes were made by actual human beings laboring in a factory. Typically these are female human beings. Was she a mother, trying to support her children? Was she a teenage girl who should have been in school but was instead laboring to keep her siblings fed? Both are likely scenarios. How much did you pay for those jeans? How much of that money do you think got back to her?

And what are you going to do with those jeans when you get tired of them, since you likely got them so cheap that they are virtually disposable? Think twice before donating them. Many people are unaware that while some of the clothes they donate are sold at secondhand stores, others are bundled into massive bales and sent overseas, where the used clothing industry has all but decimated local textile industries, putting cloth makers and tailors out of business. Sure, people get to sell the used clothes, but they make a fraction of what they would make producing beautiful clothes themselves instead of selling our castoffs. And did you know that when several East African nations attempted to raise tariffs and phase in a ban on the import of bales of not-good-enough-for-Goodwill from the United States, the United States responded by threatening to revoke certain forms of economic aid? Largely because we don't want that stuff clogging up our landfills?

Our cheap jeans are costing more than we could possibly imagine, and women and girls are picking up the tab. We can help by becoming aware of the issues and voting on how we want the world to run with our wallets. In general, we should buy less, be willing to pay more for clothing and accessories that were made in a fair, sustainable, economically healthy way, and then use our clothes until they wear out and dispose of them properly. If you're tired of your clothing but it still has a lot of wear left in it, consider organizing a clothing swap with friends or at your church, donating it to a locally owned thrift, consignment, or free store, or offloading it to a crafty friend who is into upcycling.

We are all more connected than we realize. That reality is both hopeful and terrifying, and our choices play a big role in determining which it turns out to be. If nothing else, make a practice of praying for the women who produced your clothes as you get dressed every morning. Undergarments. Shirt. Slacks. Jacket. Become conscious of the blessings we take for granted and the work of others' hands. Maybe the practice will even inspire us to give back a bit of what we have saved to women struggling to send their daughters to school.

GETTING THERE

Sometimes the hardest part about getting a girl to secondary school isn't financial—it's geographic. The reading, writing, and 'rithmitic of the primary grades can be taught by one teacher, but secondary school requires several teachers with different academic specializations. This means that while it may not be too hard to find an elementary schoolteacher to educate children in rural areas, teens often need to travel farther for high school.

This should not be unfamiliar to many of us. I live in a rural school district covering over five hundred square miles. When I was growing up, children attended small neighborhood elementary schools with anywhere from two to five classes before coming together in middle school. This only changed about twenty years ago, when the district closed all but the most far-flung tiny schools and funneled everyone else into one large elementary school. There are kids in our district who are driven half an hour or more to get to school, and the bus rides are brutal.

If that's the situation in rural America, how do families manage it in less privileged countries, especially if they don't have access to automobiles?

Boarding schools are much more common in other parts of the world than they are in the United States. It costs a lot more than enrolling your child in a local day school, but many parents prefer this option, particularly for girls. It allows them to focus on their academics without being bogged down by domestic distractions.

Other girls are sent to live with relatives in the city. Parents are typically less thrilled about this option—girls are often expected to do childcare and domestic work in exchange for room and board, and, well, I don't know many rural parents who love the idea of sending their teenage daughter to live in the city no matter how much they trust the people she is staying with. Still, for many girls, it is the only way they can get an education.

Bicycles can make a huge difference for girls who live *almost* close enough to attend a day school. Bicycles can go about ten miles per hour, going at a leisurely pace, compared to the three miles a girl could walk in the same amount of time. They also make the trip significantly safer for girls, whether they are traveling two miles or twenty. It is far easier to pedal past threats and harassment than it is to ignore or outrun them.

Bicycles have many other benefits as well, and they may be the simplest, safest, and most cost-effective way to get many adolescent girls to school. There are many nonprofits that use a variety of means to get bikes to schoolgirls. Check them out!

Of course, these are just a few of the most basic problems young women face in their pursuit of education. There are many more complex issues, including early partnering, teen pregnancy, and conflict, which create barriers that are particularly difficult for girls to navigate. We will address those in upcoming chapters.

THREE

Sex Sells

GIRLS AND COMMODIFICATION

"A patriarchal system values women as child bearers, period. So it limits their value to the time that they are sexually active, reproductively active."
—**Gloria Steinem**, *Miss Representation*

The moment I spotted Monica sitting on the other side of Mr. McCloskey's advanced eighth-grade English class, a bath towel wrapped around her hair in fulfillment of a dare, I knew we were destined to be besties. We had a lot in common. Smart, book-obsessed girls who came from deeply religious families, we had both just moved to the area from out of state. We bonded over our shared love of all things performing arts and all things 1950s. She taught me how to swing dance, I taught her how to sing harmonies, and we haunted local thrift shops searching for vintage dresses and costume jewelry. In 1990 all the other girls were sporting shoulder-length spiral perms with sky-high bangs, but both Monica and I had unreasonably long blonde hair untouched by products; she because her mother was deathly allergic to chemicals, and I because I thought ratted hair looked stupid.

We were young for our age, and advanced for our grade, and on the bottom rungs of our school's economic ladder. The special choir uniforms we were expected to buy were so out of financial reach for our families that Monica's mother bought a length of blueberry taffeta and stitched our puff-sleeved atrocities herself. The only thing that saved us from the social obliteration many of the other kids in our circle experienced was the fact that we both fit neatly into white Western standards of beauty.

It is fascinating to look back at our relationship with adult eyes. Yes, our friendship was based on shared interests, values, and a whole lot of love. But as sheltered and childlike as we were, we both had clearly become hyperaware of the social importance of being attractive to the opposite sex. We started a club, complete with our own secret code (moni floavseh byaocuk, fdleaasrh), and referred to ourselves as the Venetian Blondes. I was Venus 1, and she was Venus 2, because she was five months younger. Even the teachers played along, passing encoded notes for us when we were in different classes and occasionally referring to us by our new monikers. I suppose we were cute, and it *was* kind of funny.

Monica and I eventually developed a set of guidelines for our club: we would write one song or poem a week, kiss a boy at least once a month, and whittle our waists down to Marilyn Monroe's legendary twenty-three inches. I'm not sure we ever succeeded in those endeavors, but Monica sure kissed a lot of boys, and I developed a mild eating disorder. At least I have a journal full of angsty adolescent poetry to show for our trouble.

Monica and I were smart, outspoken girls from stable, loving families. Yet somehow we had absorbed the fact that our social power didn't lie in our intelligence, or our kindness, or our talents. It was all in our looks—particularly, in what boys and men thought about our looks. We weren't entirely wrong.

Some girls fared better than we did, and others fared worse. I'll never forget the day one of our classmates came through the door of the choir room, eyes bright red from crying. She had gone almost all the way with a boy the night before—had let him do so many things to her—and now he was trashing her all over the school. It was like a modern-day version of the tragedy of King David's daughter Tamar. There were the cheerleaders who let their boyfriends call them degrading names; the girl all the other girls despised because she wore skimpy clothes and fawned over other people's crushes; the beauties who spent more than an hour curling their hair and applying makeup every morning; and the girls who smiled and laughed in the face of boys' brutal sexual harassment, never speaking up because they wanted those same boys to think they were cool. Maybe there were girls at my school who didn't put themselves through ridiculous contortions in a bid to make themselves attractive to the opposite sex, but I'm not sure who they were. Some of this was normal teenage stuff, the very natural drive to be attractive to a potential romantic partner. Some of it was not.

These were, for the most part, relatively low-risk American girls from a wealthy school district. We haven't even touched on girls who hail from backgrounds obsessed with extreme modesty, or who are thrust into the world of beauty pageants and modeling, or who are actively sexually exploited. Our parents weren't sending us the message that we needed to be attractive in order to be loved and accepted or that it was okay for boys to treat us like sex objects. So where did those messages come from, and why did they hold such life-and-death power over us?

My guess is they were piped into our homes over the airwaves. And those messages are only getting stronger.

MEDIA AND THE BRAVE NEW WORLD

The other day I was driving a van packed to the brim with tweens and teens back to my house for a cousin sleepover. The middle schoolers got into a rapid-fire meme battle, shooting lines from their favorite viral videos back and forth like Serena Williams and Maria Sharapova at the French Open. Finally, one of them burst out, "I'm so glad there are people in my family who understand what I'm *saying*!"

I couldn't help but giggle, but she was right. Kids nowadays speak a different language from their parents because they inhabit a different world, one largely built of pixels. Growing up, I was convinced that my parents, who came of age in Nixon's era, had no idea what it was like growing up with Nirvana. But that generation gap was nothing compared to the one yawning between today's teens and their parents, who largely grew up without email and cell phones, much less YouTube, Snapchat, and online gaming. My parents at least understood the appeal of MTV. I find it incomprehensible that any kid would while away summer days watching videos of twentysomething dudes playing Minecraft in their big sister's spare bedroom.

In the 1990s, media was something we consumed. Sometime between then and now, media started consuming us. It has become an alternate universe inhabited by thumbnail-sketch avatars with carefully curated lives. I mean, I love connecting with friends on social media, but my college-age son sometimes refers to himself by his gamer tag in real life.

A 2015 study of adolescents in the United States showed that thirteen- to eighteen-year-olds consume about nine hours of media per day, including almost seven hours of screen time.[1] How do they manage this around their school, work, and extracurricular schedules, you may ask? They keep media running while doing their schoolwork, and they take their phones to bed with them. Nearly half of all teens in the United States report getting fewer than seven hours of sleep per night now, an epidemic that has soared right alongside smartphone ownership.[2] High schoolers in Japan spend over four hours a day on their phones, watching videos, playing games, and connecting on social media and messaging apps, and 43 percent of connected nine-year-olds in Brazil have social media profiles.[3] Even in Sierra Leone, where most people live on less than a dollar a day, a quarter of the population has a television at home, and 83 percent have access to a cell phone.[4]

This isn't all bad. Young people today have the world at their fingertips, and it is not only revolutionary—it has started revolutions. People are more connected and engaged with what is going on in the world than ever before, and opportunities to use media for good seem endless. However, teens primarily use the Internet for entertainment. As one Reddit user famously posted, "I possess a device, in my pocket, that is capable of accessing the entirety of information known to man. I use it to look at pictures of cats and get into arguments with strangers."[5] And of course, there are far more nefarious things on the Internet than cat memes and argumentative strangers.

THE MEDIA MALAISE

Young people may use media for entertainment, but that doesn't mean it makes them happy. Quite the opposite. A 2017 study by the University of Michigan shows that self-esteem among American teens, which had been on the upswing since the early 1990s, began to plummet in 2012, when smartphone ownership passed the 50 percent mark.[6] In the five years between 2010 and 2015, teen suicide attempts jumped 23 percent, and actual suicides increased by 31 percent.[7] This phenomenon cut across every social, ethnic, and economic category, but one group was particularly affected: girls.[8] In fact, suicides among teen girls rose an astonishing 65 percent.[9]

Social media, which girls use at much higher rates than boys, is particularly problematic.[10] We know that consistent exposure to images promoting unrealistic standards of beauty can do great damage to a woman's psyche. But when you are a teenager, it's hard to resist constantly checking in on the carefully curated, artistically staged, and heavily filtered photos of your classmates living their best lives. Many teens and young adults readily admit that scrolling through their social feeds is depressing, making them anxious that their lives compare poorly with their peers' Instagram stories.[11] Others fear being called out because their real lives are not as interesting or glamorous as they portray on social media. And yet, like addicts, they report feeling unable to stop. In

American Girls: Social Media and the Secret Lives of Teenagers, Nancy Jo Sales recounts a conversation with three teenage girls, one of whom insisted that social media was destroying their lives. When asked why they didn't go off it, another girl responded, "Because then we would have no life."[12] American teenage girls spend about an hour and a half falling down the rabbit hole of social media each day.[13]

SEXTING, BROGRAMMERS, AND KEEPING UP WITH THE KARDASHIANS

Let's be clear about something. Social media is not a neutral space. Nor are magazines, television channels, movie studios, or recording labels. It is no secret to people in those industries that images of women who have been photoshopped and airbrushed out of the realm of reality make women feel bad about themselves and make men feel really, really good. Advertisers depend on both of those things to sell their products.

So why not make men feel insecure and make women feel good? We are beginning to see a bit more of that, with the bumbling dad trope in television and advertising—although those bumbling dads are typically fully clothed and look a lot more like average men than their female counterparts. It's apples and oranges. No, the reason the media is so obsessed with sexualized, idealized fantasy women is twofold. First, women have traditionally been viewed as existing for the benefit of men, and we are all so used to those insidious messages that we don't even notice them. Second, most of the advertisers, studio heads, and decision-makers in media are male. Even Silicon Valley, which one would expect to be more progressive, is notorious for its treatment of women.

An article in *The Atlantic* titled "Silicon Valley Is a Big Ole Fraternity" sums it up nicely before you even get to the text. It's worth reading, though, as it succinctly explains the rise of "brogrammers"—and questions whether dubbing their rare female counterparts "hogrammers" is really a move toward greater inclusion for women.[14] These are the people building the sites and creating the media our youth spend more than half their waking hours engaged in.

But aren't there women working in media too? And aren't female actors, models, and even female writers, producers, and executives willingly engaging in this supposedly degrading work? Yes and yes—for the most part, at least. But the question we must pose as Christ-followers committed to the welfare of young women is not whether some women are surviving and thriving in male-dominated systems. Some women have always done very well for themselves in male-dominated systems, particularly if they are pretty, savvy, and well connected.

The question is who the system was created for, who benefits, and who pays the price. In the United States and Canada, it is typically the media companies and advertisers who benefit, and the women who pay the price.

PORNIFICATION

Several years back, I noticed some of my mom friends posting pictures of themselves in bikinis. Not pictures of them vacationing at the beach, or relaxing poolside, or playing in the sprinklers with their kids, all situations in which two-piece swimsuits may be a very practical choice. They were just flat out wearing bikinis and posting pictures of themselves to social media.

I might have scrolled right past these photos of thirty-something women sitting cross-legged in kiddie pools had it not been for the captions. Apparently, there was some sort of quasi-feminist social media challenge going on—they wrote about their repressive upbringings, the shame they carried about their bodies, and how they were finally breaking free. Which is great! But is jumping on a social media bandwagon that is encouraging you to post bikini pics really the best way to declare your independence from the patriarchy? And why were the very slender or very busty women the only ones who seemed to find this empowering?

Okay, look. I'm not judging anyone's swimwear. (Except when I am—like when parents dress little girls in skimpy, sexualized swimwear. Then I'm totally judging.) I wore my share of bikinis in my teens and twenties, and still wear a modest two-piece when I'm hanging out at the beach with my kids. But I don't fold laundry, or write, or walk my dog in a swimsuit to prove that I am comfortable with my body. That wouldn't benefit me. My husband might like it (or more likely, would become deeply concerned about my emotional well-being), but the only benefit I can see in wearing a swimsuit with no water or sun in sight is to feel sexy. And for the record, *sexy* means sexually attractive. To someone else. Meaning, it's about how others see you, not how you see yourself.

It's fun to feel sexy, in the right context. Our sexuality is part of who we are, part of how God created us. But the reason women so often equate sexiness with empowerment is because making oneself attractive to men has, historically, been the most effective way—and sometimes the only way—to gain power in male-dominant systems.

It's all for the male gaze, y'all. Maybe we're not doing it directly for men—maybe we're doing it to bolster our own self-esteem, or to impress other women, or even to show our legalistic parents that they're not the boss of us anymore. But isn't it interesting that we express that by stripping down and declaring ourselves desirable? As Dana Carvey's old *Saturday Night Live* Church Lady character would say, "How conveeeeenient."

Unfortunately, the next generation of girls—and boys—has been watching and learning. And not only from their mothers. They've been learning from movie stars, and Instagram icons, and reality TV (shudder), and music videos. And yep, they've been learning from porn, which is not only readily available to young people nowadays but almost impossible to avoid. In fact, pornographic norms are slipping into the mainstream. We may joke about the sultry faces that young women make in selfies, but where do those expressions *come* from? Where did thirteen-year-old girls learn that if they want to look hot, they should plump and purse their lips and leave their mouths slightly open?

In *American Girls*, Sales writes about the enormous pressure young women feel nowadays to be "sex positive," which often loosely translates into being cool with porn, posting sexy pictures of themselves online, and not getting offended by requests for sexual favors. "A boy will ask you to [give oral sex], and if you say no, then you're a prude, but then when you actually do it, you're a slut," one girl explained. Another explained that it was best to laugh off inappropriate requests, because "if you get mad, they'll think you have no chill. . . . They judge you if you don't send nudes, like you're a prude. But if you just laugh, then they'll be aggravated, but they won't do anything bad to you."[15]

Young women today are not just expected to objectify themselves; they are expected to do it with a smile—or a plump-lipped porn pout—and call it empowering. That's not empowerment. That's the classic Tom Sawyer con, and we're paying dearly for the privilege of playing his game.

SONG OF SONGS

There are some confusing books in the Bible, but in keeping with its name, Song of Songs tops them all. No one seems quite sure what to do with it. Is it an allegory describing the relationship between God and Israel or Christ and the church? Is it a drama describing the relationship between two lovers, or a love triangle in which King Solomon tries to woo a country girl away from the shepherd boy she loves? Is it a collection of love poems read at wedding celebrations, or a cultic holdover from pagan religions?

Whatever else it is, it is certainly a celebration of the romantic love enjoyed between a woman and a man. The woman's unabashed frankness about her sexual desires, and the role her mother and the "daughters of Jerusalem" play in advancing her relationship with her beloved, is especially startling to readers accustomed to viewing women as prizes to be pursued, given away, and enjoyed by men. It all seems a bit scandalous, from that perspective, which is probably why millennia's worth of scholars have gone through so many contortions to allegorize it or explain it away. But the Shulammite woman is not the least bit afraid or ashamed of her sexuality. There are hints in the text at the threats posed by men—angry brothers, other shepherds, and violent watchmen—but the heroine refuses to allow those things to hinder her pursuit of her beloved.

Three times, however, the Shulammite interrupts her own monologues with a poignant plea. She asks that the daughters of Jerusalem not "arouse or awaken love until it so desires" (Song of Songs 2:7, 3:5, 8:4). The delights of emotional and physical intimacy in a loving, mutual relationship turn sour when forced—when the girl is too young, or unready to leave her family's home, or simply does not desire that sort of relationship. The Shulammite is so adamant about this that she wants the women to swear an oath—not by the holy objects one might expect, but "by the gazelles and by the does of the field" (Song of Songs 3:5): beautiful, fleet-footed creatures who expertly avoid capture. J. Cheryl Exum points out that in Hebrew, the words for "gazelles" and "does of the field" look and sound like Hebrew names for God, cleverly drawing them into the realm of the feminine.[16] These words added weight to the unconventional oath without committing sacrilege or formalizing it in a way the temple or the family patriarch could meddle with.

Three thousand years later, the Shulammite's plea still resonates deeply. It brings to mind the sacred pacts of girlhood—the whispered secrets, woven bracelets, and halves of heart-shaped necklaces exchanged to solemnize our understanding of our relationships. It echoes the unspoken sisterhood of adult women as well—the way we show up when Mom gets cancer, or our sister's husband is being difficult, or our friend is in crisis. Not every woman has been lucky enough to experience those sorts of relationships, and betrayals of those relationships are some of the most painful to navigate, whether we are children or adults. But the undercurrent of women bonding together to avoid being swept away by the unfriendly tides of a patriarchal world has flowed throughout history, and it is a beautiful, countercultural force.

What if we responded to the Shulammite's request? What if we agreed, by the gazelles and by the does of the field, that we will not allow our daughters, or anyone else's daughters, to be sexualized? What if we promised, like the caring adults of Song of Songs 8, to be a battlement of silver protecting their walls until they declare themselves ready to venture beyond them, cedar boards shielding their vulnerable areas until they are ready to unlatch their doors themselves?

An important distinction needs to be made here. Female virginity has been commodified for millennia, a symbol of a father's honor that could be sold to the highest bidder when he deemed the time right. That is the antithesis of what I am suggesting. Purity culture, with its focus on "saving yourself" for your future spouse, can be as detrimental to a young woman's well-being as hook-up culture. Both are symptoms of a hypersexual mindset that puts too much weight on a girl's sexuality and too little on her personhood.

To be clear, I believe that the Bible teaches abstinence outside of marriage. But we should abstain to honor God with our choices, not to honor a future spouse with our bodies, or because some youth pastor promised it will make our married sex lives better. The "True Love Waits" campaign began when I was in high school, and a few of my friends were given abstinence rings, to remind them of their commitment to be faithful to their future spouse. I don't think it's a bad idea to have a tangible reminder of your religious commitments (altars served a similar purpose for the ancient Israelites), but I think it's a very bad idea—an idolatrous idea, even—to focus those commitments on a human being. Those parents would have been better off giving their children a cross to remind them of their commitment to be faithful to Jesus, not so that he will bless us with marital bliss somewhere down the road, but because Jesus is God, and he is good, and he is owed our allegiance. Besides, if we teach our youth that coming to the marriage bed as a virgin is the end goal, where does that leave young women who have had sex? Or who have been raped? Or who never marry at all and feel they never received what they were promised? Nowhere good.

Taken to its extreme, this obsession with female virginity is the force behind honor killings and the idea that a woman is "ruined" if she has sex, consensual or otherwise. Ruined for what? Not for sexual intimacy or childbearing, in all but the most extreme cases. No, she has been ruined for sale as a virgin, and the fact that her body slipped from the clutches of her father's or potential future husband's control lessens her perceived value in a patriarchal system. It's a crass mindset in which human beings created in the image of God are treated like automobiles on a car lot, their value determined by the prestige the purchaser has been conditioned to feel in ownership, and the price they can bring their seller. But praise God, our value is not in our bodies. God is concerned about the purity of our hearts, not what the world deems the "purity" of our bodies. We need to take a good, hard look at where our ideas about sexuality come from, hold them up to the light of Scripture and the life of Christ, and reorient our actions and attitudes accordingly.

Certainly, parents and mentors are responsible to help young women make wise, God-honoring choices about how they express their sexuality. But we need to protect their innocence as well, shielding their heart and mind from the weight of other people's sexuality. And that is no easy task in this day and age.

DO NOT AROUSE OR AWAKEN LOVE UNTIL IT SO DESIRES

A while back, I flouted every rule of polite conversation and put a question out on Facebook: "How old were you when you realized people might look at you in a sexual way, and how did that make you feel?"

There was the Internet equivalent of an awkward pause, and then the responses began to pour in.

Brittany was in fourth grade when she realized her body could draw attention, and by middle school, she was leveraging it as a form of social power among her peers. She and her friends would don makeup and skimpy clothes to see how many honks they could get while walking to the local dollar store. Although Brittany remained celibate until marriage and didn't even kiss a boy until college, being "hot" increased her cool factor with her female friends.

Abigail was sexually abused at age four and became preoccupied with sex as a result. She swung between hiding her body under boys' clothing, certain God had made a dire mistake in making her a girl, and trying to gain attention for her body through starvation, self-harm, and kissing lots of people. She was eight when she came to believe that she "would always be looked at as an object."

Melody confided that she was forty-four before she realized someone might find her desirable. By the time she hit puberty at eleven, she was firmly entrenched in the dieting cycle, "trying to gain lovability by becoming smaller—and not succeeding." If there were boys who flirted with her, she ignored it. "When the messages of one's exclusion are so consistent, complete, and profound, it can be extremely risky to imply in any minute way that one believes it is possible to be a part. Imagine the tried-and-true teen movie scene where the unpopular girl's ultimate humiliation is that she actually *believed* that the cute football player would ask her to the dance!"

Catherine summed the experience of many girls up nicely:

My first awareness came through harassment from boys around my age (who, looking back on it, must have been pretty broken to have such ideas so young) when I was eleven, twelve, and thirteen. This came in the form of speculative comments about my vagina, what it would be like to do various things to me and my friends, and actual actions: trying to force girls' shirts up over their heads at recess so boys could take off their bras and touch their breasts, boys pulling down their pants on the bus in front of girls' faces to imply oral sex, etc. All this was *years* before I could conceive of such an activity as desirable, and obviously never in such a demeaning way. So I associated my first experiences of being a "sex object" as something dangerous and devaluing, that I tried to protect myself from.

But all around me were messages that said plainly that the way to have value was to dress, look, and talk in a way that welcomed this treatment, and to my surprise, it seemed that as time went on, many girls my age accepted this message and went with it. So from about age thirteen to age sixteen, I had these two conflicting layers: You are seen as a sex object, which is dangerous and devaluing, but the only way to have any value is to embrace this and put most of your time, money, and identity into cultivating this. If you fail, you will not have value.

I was twelve years old when I realized, much to my horror, that men might look at me in ways I did not want them to look at me. I must have had some understanding of this before—I knew about good touch and bad touch, I remember my mother instructing me to close the curtains before I changed, and since I spent much of my childhood in West Africa, where it wasn't uncommon for girls to be spoken for when they were very young, I knew there were men who might want to "date" me, even though I was just a kid. But it didn't sink in until we moved back to the States. A series of unfortunate events—involving a military caravan and a stonewashed denim skirt set my "cool" auntie had given me—led to a conversation with my parents about why smiling at people could give them the wrong idea, and why certain outfits just shouldn't be worn by girls who had the misfortune of looking older than they actually were.

I was horrified. In fact, I would go so far as to say that this realization was traumatic, and that it played into the eating disorder I developed later. That eating disorder was a not-so-subtle attempt to keep my body firmly under my own control and mold it into conformity with norms I felt were safe and beneficial.

To this day I am not sure what, if anything, my parents could have done differently. Providing girls with the information they need to keep themselves safe in a hypersexualized society—all without frightening them or allowing the weight of other people's sexuality to land on their underdeveloped shoulders—is no small task. The world can be an ugly place, and waking up to those realities as our brains develop the ability to perceive them is one of the unpleasant parts of growing up. But if we can't find some way to do this better, we need to at least stop making it worse.

RETIRING THE MODESTY POLICE

"I don't care what she was wearing! She's a college student, coming to church. They should just be thankful she showed up!"

I was livid. My husband, who was serving as a worship pastor at the time, had recruited a young woman attending the local college to sing on the worship team the past Sunday. She had done a great job, but my husband had just endured an all-male elders' meeting that included a long conversation about the young woman's slacks. They were too tight. They were too light-colored. Someone would have to talk with her. Men are very visual, you see, and tight slacks could lead them into sin.

I'm just gonna come out and say this. Any time you have a group of fifty-year-old men sitting around discussing a twenty-year-old's dress slacks, it's not the young woman who's the problem. And you want to talk about leading people into sin? Ooh, lead me not into temptation, brothers! Because that sort of arrogant, entitled, sexist nonsense—especially when aimed at the young—leads me right to the edge of patience, kindness, goodness, faithfulness, gentleness, and self-control.

Even if the clothing *was* a problem—if, say, she had shown up in fishnets, booty shorts, and six-inch heels—I would expect men of God old enough to be her father to express concern about *her*, and to make a discreet inquiry about her well-being, not sit around having a conversation about male virility and how men might be affected by her wardrobe choices.

Pull it together, guys. We need you to be better than that.

The church is bad at talking about sex. And by that I don't mean we don't talk about it enough. Quite frankly, I could die happy never having had a conversation about sex with most of the pastors I know. I mean that when we do talk about it, we often don't do it well. In fact, the messages that the church sends people about sexuality often bear a striking resemblance to the messages the media sends us, and to similar effect. Men are really into sex (high fives all around!), so women need to dress for the male gaze the way they'd dress for a storm. If you're too pretty, men will prey on you. If you're too schlubby, you'll be written off. Either way, it's your fault, because the responsibility for managing male sexuality has been projected onto your female shoulders. (Which you should definitely never show, unless you're, like, taking a pole dancing class so you can dance for your husband. And yes, that is a real thing I heard a real pastor talking about at a real church I visited once. Not impressed by Pastor Dude-Bro's edginess.) Once again, men are made to feel powerful, and women are made to feel insecure.

One of the problems inherent in addressing the sexualization of girls is that it really belongs in a book for and about men and boys. Sure, women sometimes participate in their own sexualization. In a male-dominated society, being sexually appealing to men provides a certain level of social and even economic power. It can also serve as a convenient mask, a distraction to keep people from seeing what is under the surface. And yes, women are even more likely than men to serve as "modesty police"—or at least that has been the case at most of the churches in which I have been involved. It makes them feel powerful too. But it is still all about the male gaze.

Friends, the centrality of the male gaze—the importance ascribed to the way men view women—has been elevated beyond all sense. The church, the media, and the world have, in many ways, trained women to be more concerned about how men view them than about how they view themselves. A Christian book that came out a while back shot to the top of the bestseller charts on the claim that the deepest desire of the female heart is to be, as summed up in its one-word title, *captivating*. I haven't read the book and thus can offer no critique, but the title alone should give us pause. Where have we come to as a society when it makes sense to us that a woman's deepest longing relates to how others *perceive* her? Say that women, like men, desire to be loved. Of course they do! We were all created to be the object of God's love. Say that women desire to be captivating—as in, their captivating-ness is the subject of the sentence, and men and God are the objects they desire to captivate? Um, no. Just no.

I'm not saying it's not true, in many cases. In fact, I've known plenty of women who were more in love with the idea of being loved than they were with the man who actually loved them. This is terribly dehumanizing for the man and tragic for everyone involved. No, what I am saying is that it's idolatry: culturally ingrained idolatry, which tells women that their value comes not from who they are—created in the image of a captivating God, who deserves all glory, honor, and praise—but from how others perceive them.

In short, women have been trained to think far more highly than they ought about whether men perceive them far more highly than they ought.

But back to modesty and lust.

Let's take the logic that many churches apply to lust several steps further: to sexual assault. Leaving aside for a moment the fact that some men are victims and some women are perpetrators, is sexual assault primarily a women's issue or a men's issue? To hear us talk about it, you'd think it is a women's issue. But it's not, is it? Men are the ones who are committing assault. Men are the ones who are sinning against their sisters. It's a men's issue. They are creating a problem for women, of course, but it is a problem that stems from male behavior, not female behavior.

Why, then, do we focus so much energy on telling women to change their behavior to avoid being assaulted instead of telling men to change their behavior and stop assaulting women? By the same token, why are we telling women to check their hemlines to avoid being made an object of lust instead of telling men to check their hearts and, in the words of my teens, "quit acting like creepers?"

I will tell you why. Because it's not actually about modesty. It's about power and control.

Don't misunderstand me. I don't believe that women (or men) should dress in a way that is meant to attract sexual attention, unless they are alone with their spouse. Maybe it's my missionary background coming out, but I don't believe people should dress in a way that is meant to draw attention to themselves, period, whether they're showing off designer duds or virtue signaling with denim jumpers. Wear beautiful clothes, experiment with color, cut, and texture, delight in something new and fun, but if your primary motivation in getting dressed in the morning has to do with attracting other people's attention, it may be a warning sign that something in your emotional life needs tending.

But modesty is subjective. It is not about what people wear; it is about how it is perceived. Think about what women wore before Western modes of dress were normalized. In some places, it was little more than a length of cloth, string, or plant fibers wrapped around their midsection, while in others, they were literally covered head to toe. What was the difference? Were men in less-clothed cultures less susceptible to lust than men in cultures where women were heavily veiled? Of course not. People just decided what was acceptable to them and acted in accordance with the prevailing social norms.

Which means, men, that you have some level of choice in how you respond to women in various forms of dress and undress. That you can train yourselves to see women as sisters, not sex objects. Sure, we all have natural inclinations, but we do not need to be controlled by them or use them as an excuse to control others. Your morality is not at the mercy of women's wardrobe choices. Please, think carefully before placing the weight of your sexuality on anyone else's shoulders, particularly if those shoulders happen to belong to someone young and female. She doesn't need to be weighed down by your lust.

In summary: women, quit obsessing; men, quit being creepers; parents, quit letting your kids sleep with their phones.

Got it? Good. Let's move on.

FOUR

The Oldest Injustice

GIRLS AND GENDER-BASED VIOLENCE

Sahar Gul shot into the spotlight when she was rescued by Afghan police in 2011. Sold into marriage at twelve, her in-laws tried to force her into prostitution. When she refused, they locked her in the basement, where she endured months of torture at the hands of the entire family. Her own family became concerned when their attempts to visit her were rebuffed, and they finally called the authorities. Photos of the battered girl prompted outrage in Afghanistan and around the world, and Sahar became the first victim of domestic violence in that country to be represented by an attorney.

Sahar's case may have been extreme, but the only thing unique about it is that she attained some modicum of justice.

Seattle-based pastor and social entrepreneur Eugene Cho, blogging about Sahar's case and many others like it, said that "the oldest injustice in human history is the way we treat women."[1] He is right. Oppression and its handmaiden, violence, have stalked females in every culture, in every time. From acid attacks in India to weaponized rape in DR Congo to femicide in Brazil to trafficking in Thailand, untold numbers of women and girls are subjected to violence for the simple fact that they were born female.

Gender-based violence isn't just a problem "out there." Between 2001 and 2012, 6,488 American troops were killed in Afghanistan. During that same period, 11,766 American women were murdered by intimate partners.[2] That's about three murders per day. One in four women has experienced severe physical violence at the hands of an intimate partner; one in six has been sexually violated; and one in seven has been stalked—all by someone who claimed to love them.[3] Overall, somewhere between a third and a fourth of American women have experienced sexual abuse or assault at the hands of a relative, acquaintance, or stranger before turning eighteen. While it is notoriously difficult to get exact numbers on this, a variety of studies involving both adult and adolescent subjects consistently come up with similar numbers.[4]

Age is a significant factor in gender-based violence. In fact, since most nations do not consider people legal adults until they are eighteen, and the human brain isn't fully developed until about twenty-five, it might be more accurate to say that the oldest injustice in human history is the way we treat *girls*, particularly adolescent and post-adolescent females between the ages of twelve and twenty-four. A report from the Centers for Disease Control pointed out that when you lump together all the forms of abuse they were tracking, most of it occurred or began before the victim turned twenty-five. This is the case for nearly 80 percent of rape survivors: 12 percent of them were first victimized at age ten or younger, 28 percent between the ages of eleven and seventeen, and 38 percent between eighteen and twenty-four. Rates of intimate partner violence are highest among women between the ages of eighteen and twenty-four, and if crimes against underage girls were not treated differently by the legal system, sixteen- and seventeen-year-olds could be included in that category as well. Seventy-one percent of domestic violence survivors were first abused before they turned twenty-five, compared to 21 percent of victims for whom the abuse began between the ages of twenty-five and thirty-four, 6 percent between the ages of thirty-five and forty-four, and 2 percent at age forty-five and above.[5] The widespread maxim that if you have four women in a room, one of them has probably been abused holds true. However, there is a high likelihood that woman was a girl when it happened.

Practically speaking, this means we have significant work to do when it comes to educating our youth about gender-based violence. It is encouraging that rates of abuse tend to drop off as people become older and wiser, but it should never happen in the first place. What are our girls and boys learning or not learning under our care that is putting them at such high risk for becoming victims or perpetrators of violence?

OH BOY

As the mother of four sons, and as a foster parent, I take this issue very seriously. Much of the last chapter was spent discussing the social pressures that make girls vulnerable, but let's switch our focus and talk for a minute about how we raise boys. If you recall, violence against women is not primarily a women's issue. It is a men's issue. If we want the world to become safer for females, we need to raise principled, nonviolent males who will be part of the solution, not part of the problem.

Children tend to model the actions and attitudes they learn in their homes. They take their cues about what is right and wrong, appropriate and inappropriate, acceptable and unacceptable, from the people who raise them: primarily their parents, but siblings and extended family members play a role in this as well. As children get older, the world outside the walls of their homes gains more influence, but the family is still the foundational social unit, the subconscious scaffolding on which we build our other relationships. We can do the hard work of digging up those old foundations and laying a new course for our life, of course, and some young people do dangerously veer off the good foundation their parents laid. But for the most part, we learn our values, expectations, and behaviors at home.

One in fifteen American children grows up in a home in which domestic violence is occurring, and 90 percent of those young people have been eyewitnesses to the violence.[6] It should come as no surprise to anyone that this has a destructive impact on children's lives, whether the abuser ever lays a hand on them or not. People who grew up in violent homes are 50 percent more likely to abuse drugs and alcohol, six times more likely to commit suicide, fifteen times more likely to be physically or sexually assaulted, and 74 percent more likely to commit a violent crime themselves.[7] Growing up in a violent household is the best predictor for whether children will repeat the cycle they witnessed at home in their own families, either as victims or as perpetrators.[8] The damage is catastrophic.

But a child does not have to grow up with violence to learn disdain. Mockery and casual cruelty teach children that there is social collateral to be gained in antagonizing others. Excusing such behavior as "joking" teaches children that the victim's voice is less important than the perpetrator's and will likely be dismissed to keep everyone else comfortable. (Seriously, if I had a quarter for every time a young man complained to me about someone calling out their nonsense, "tattling," criticizing, or getting angry at them for their inappropriate behavior, I would be a wealthy, wealthy woman. The problem is not someone mentioning the problem, boys; the problem is the problem.) Sexist comments and reinforced stereotypes give children cues on how their mentors believe people should behave. If a father consistently rolls his eyes when the mother makes a request, or a mother walks on eggshells to accommodate the father's moods, children will assume that is how men and women are supposed to interact. And while a forty-five-year-old man—one who rants about how that girl on the news was obviously asking for it, going to that party in that dress and acting that way—may have the common sense *not* to assault inebriated young women in skimpy clothing, his nineteen-year-old son may take his father at his word and act accordingly.

We need to pave a better path for our boys, brick by brick, choice by choice, conversation by conversation, right action by right action. Not because we're trying to be "politically correct," whatever that means, but because we are trying to raise respectful young men of integrity, who do the right thing even when they don't have to.

NAMING THE PROBLEM BEFORE IT BECOMES A PROBLEM

Doug sat on the sofa across from me in the beautiful, rustic addition he had built onto the cabin he shared with Bonnie, who was curled up at his side. I had known Bonnie my whole life, but I hadn't been aware of how troubled her marriage to Doug was until years after they sought help, and went public with their story in an attempt to help others. Doug had never hit Bonnie or her sons, but he would become emotionally and verbally abusive when he got stressed. Finally, Bonnie drew the line, and Doug agreed to get help.

Luckily, they lived in the right area. Doug went through the groundbreaking nonviolence training offered by Duluth's Domestic Abuse Intervention Program—a six-month class focused on creating a process of change for men who batter. Most of the men who attend the class are court ordered to be there, and an astonishing 70 percent of them are never arrested for domestic assault again.[9] It's a transformative program, and it rocked the foundations of Doug's world, pulling them down and putting something better in their place. After graduating from the class, he went through training to become a co-facilitator, helping others find the healing he himself received.

Doug explained that a huge part of his own rehabilitation and recovery was learning to recognize his feelings and respond to them appropriately. He had grown up in a violent home, and as a boy, the only emotions it was safe to express were dominant, powerful ones like rage. Everything else had to be stuffed down or expressed in an alternative way. Therefore, anger had become his default response to any painful emotional stimuli. Loneliness manifested as rage. Grief manifested as rage. Exhaustion, frustration, disappointment, uncertainty—rage, rage, rage, rage. He had to retrain himself to stop, spend some time thinking about what he was actually feeling, and determine what a healthy, adult response to that feeling would be.

I fear this is the case for many of our boys, whether they grow up in violent homes or not. We live in a fast-paced, reactive culture that disdains weakness, especially from men. By the time boys hit preschool, they have already learned that boys are expected to be tough and that there are social consequences to crying when they are hurt or clinging when they are afraid. Of course, all children need to learn to manage their emotions in healthy ways, but we teach boys to manifest a stoic indifference to their own pain—to "walk it off," physically and emotionally—in a way that walls them off from their own experiences and makes it clear that the performance of masculinity is more important than heeding feelings and tending to wounds. This is a convenient skill to have when your village is being invaded by a Viking horde. It is less useful when trying to understand why your female coworker is so upset about that comment you made at staff meeting, or how to help your teenage son navigate his disappointment about the girl he likes wanting to remain "just friends."

So how can adults do better by our boys? We can begin by naming the feelings they seem to be manifesting and helping them think through the appropriate response. Instead of telling a crying child to "be a big boy" when dropping him off at a new daycare, we can say "I know you feel nervous, but they will take good care of you, and I will be back to pick you up at dinnertime." When they act up, we can say "I understand that you feel frustrated, but it is not polite to yell" or "It is okay to feel angry, but it is never okay to hit." This does not mean that we cave in to the child's demands or cede parental authority; it is just a simple way to teach children how to recognize their feelings and what an appropriate response to those feelings would be.

It is best to start this early, but it is never too late to begin, even if you have to contend with a bit of eye-rolling. Amp up your emotional vocabulary in your conversations with teen boys. "Wow, that sounds disappointing" and "That stinks—I would feel hurt if my friend said that" are easy ways to equip teens with the tools they need to recognize, navigate, and manage their emotional landscape. One of my teenage foster sons became obsessed with the word *miffed*. He'd grin and ask, "Jenny, are you miffed?" or stop in the middle of a stressful situation and yell, "I'm feeling very miffed!"—still with a huge grin on his face. He thought the word was hilarious, but that grin came from the relief of realizing that frustration, annoyance, and irritation didn't always have to escalate into rage and retribution. That sometimes, people could just be miffed, and that was okay.

It is also important to have conversations with boys (and girls) about consent, and what is and is not appropriate. It can feel awkward, sure, but it needs to be done. Kids don't necessarily know where the lines fall, or why. This is especially true if they have seen those lines crossed, in the media or in real life, or if their own boundaries have been violated in large or small ways.

Start early by modeling consent with your children. Don't make them hug or kiss people they don't want to hug or kiss, and if you are wrestling, tickling, or roughhousing, always stop immediately when your child says "Stop," even if you are not sure they mean it. This teaches them that their no will be respected and that they should respect other people's no as well. Have matter-of-fact conversations with elementary schoolers about keeping their hands to themselves, with middle schoolers about what bullying and harassment look like, and with high schoolers about how to manage physical and relational boundaries as they grow into adult bodies and relationships.

Let's hang out on that transition from tween to adult bodies for a moment. We all know that growth spurts can make children clumsy and awkward, but we often forget that there is a social and emotional aspect to this as well, especially when a boy who wore children's sizes a few months ago wakes up one day towering over his mama. His mental and emotional development may have kept pace with his body, or it may not have. In either case, boys in this phase are suddenly walking through the world in a whole new way, whether they are aware of it or not. My sons are big kids—my twelve-year-old is the only one who hasn't topped six feet yet—and in my experience, it is very common for boys to need a little advice about how to manage their new adult-sized bodies. So my husband and I remind them to take their new size and strength into account when playing, arguing, and roughhousing, especially with friends or siblings who haven't hit that phase yet. Arm wrestling matches, with dad and with one another, are a fun way to keep this in the forefront of their minds. We teach them to angle their bodies and stand a bit to the side of people, because few things in life are more intimidating than a 6-foot, 3-inch behemoth staring down at you while blocking your path—even if they are only talking about how they *really need* you to drive them to Dollar General to get butterscotch chips for the cookies they promised to bake for their choir buddies. We make sure they know that they should avoid walking directly behind a female—that they should move to the side and pass her if possible, so she knows they are not following her. How would a young man know that if no one told him? And we stress the fact that strength is a gift meant to build people, places, and things up, never a tool to be leveraged to control or do violence.

Sometimes these conversations are intense, sometimes they are funny, and most of the time they are just matter-of-fact reminders—life hacks that help our boys avoid misunderstanding and communicate well with others.

WHEN VIOLENCE FEELS NATURAL: ON DRAWING THE LINE, AND HOLDING IT

I was standing in the hallway of the assisted-living home, sandwiched between my grandma Vivien and a tiny, agitated woman who was picking at the band around her wrist. The woman lived in the room next to my grandmother, but she often forgot that fact. By the time she had pushed her walker past my grandmother's open door the fourth time, we decided we had better help her out. I phoned the front desk and asked them to bring up a set of keys, while my grandmother assured her that she was in the right place and attempted to distract her with pleasant conversation. "Attempted" is the key word here.

To understand my grandmother, you need to understand that she was, at her core, a pastor. She completed Salvation Army officer training right out of high school and functioned in that capacity until her dying day, whether she was wearing the uniform or not. So like any good pastor, she took what she knew about the woman and attempted to engage with her about a topic she knew she was interested in—in this case, the big ships that glided in and out of Duluth's harbor. Apparently, the woman would stand at the large window at the end of the hallway for hours on end, watching for them. There was nothing particularly unusual about this; lots of people like to watch the ships come in, and tourists often plan their schedules around the arrival of certain ocean liners. When the ships did arrive, however, the woman would become very agitated, certain she needed to get dressed up and go down to the docks for parties with the sailors.

My grandma smiled like this was cute, but my jaw dropped in horror. In Duluth, "party on the boats" is a euphemism for a certain form of prostitution that has affected generations of women. Native women from the nearby reservations were particularly vulnerable—they would be bundled onto the ships, where they would service sailors bound for destinations all over the world. Many of them never made it home. But apparently, this frail, fretful woman was one of the ones who had.

Most people don't look at a confused elderly woman and think "trafficking survivor," or visit assisted-living facilities expecting to have conversations about sexual assault. But with my grandma, it was becoming par for the course. She had never been particularly secretive about the sexual abuse in her own background. It was hard to hide, since she had given birth at sixteen, and even in the 1940s it had been clear that the relationship was not consensual. But the depth of what she had survived didn't begin to come out until the last decade or so of her life, after most of the people involved had died.

Conversations became particularly distressing in her last year, when the onset of dementia began to corrode the filters in her mind and traumas from her past got jumbled together with situations in her daily life. Violence, false imprisonment, and missing babies featured heavily in her stories about what she believed to be happening in other people's lives. She was desperate to save the women she believed to be in danger— she would call friends and family members, trying to enlist their help, and would lay small, soft blankets on her bed, ready to receive the infants she thought the women had given birth to. When the imaginary babies didn't show up, she would become convinced something horrible had happened to them and would grieve. It was brutal.

But the thing that struck me most was something my grandmother said before the dementia kicked in. As a young woman, she had believed molestation, rape, and sexual aggression were "just what men do." She had experienced so much abuse, from so many different quarters, that she accepted it as completely normal. It took cataclysmic events— such as becoming pregnant or being locked in a motel room far from home—to even register on her "something's not right; I need to find help" scale. Otherwise, she just did her best to survive.

And therein lies a large part of the problem. Violence against women is so common that it doesn't even register as a significant problem—until it crosses whatever invisible line an individual or society has drawn. When emotional abuse turns physical. When groping moves under the clothing. When bruises turn into broken bones. When penetration occurs. Once that invisible line has been crossed, there are only a few options: you can live with the horror, or try to change things, or push the line further back so you can maintain the illusion that everything is still okay.

Unfortunately, society often chooses to push the line further back. Personally, I don't think it is because people are uncaring monsters. I think it is because they aren't sure how to address the situation, and trying to is extremely awkward. Yes, awkward. Who wants to ask about something so personal, make a scene about something so humiliating, or accuse someone of behavior ranging from really inappropriate to downright depraved?

Perpetrators are aware of this awkwardness and take full advantage of it. They count on no one expressing discomfort about how their interactions with children seem just a little too friendly, because they are a pillar of the church. They count on young women being "too polite" to snarl or ram their elbow into their ribs when they press too close in crowded areas. They count on being too loved, or too charismatic, or too important for anyone to call them out on their shadow side—or for any accusations against them to stick if they do. They count on plausible deniability, on public opinion being in their favor, on the manufactured outrage they can summon when accused, on their victims feeling that speaking up might just make matters worse for them. Grooming is all about pushing the line back. And it is not just the victims who are groomed. It is society.

For others, pushing the line back is a coping mechanism that allows them to maintain their sanity in horrific circumstances. A woman once told me that it was easier to believe that she hadn't actually been raped—that she had played some part in a man forcing his way into her home and brutalizing her—because admitting how powerless she had been in that situation was more terrifying than any shame she could conjure up about imaginary complicity. Another woman, when asked why she hadn't left her abuser, looked in disbelief at the person asking her this and said, "Because he said he'd kill me and the kids if we left." Death threats are a compelling reason to keep your head down. And what about the girls who have no place to turn: who don't feel safe at home, church, or school and who have no reason to believe anyone will help them? Minimization and denial are powerful coping mechanisms, especially when you don't see any way to change your circumstances.

Sometimes I wonder how my great-grandma Eleanor, my grandma Vivien's mother, survived. By all accounts she was not a nice woman. The scion of a wealthy East Coast family, she struggled to maintain appearances while raising nine children during the Great Depression on whatever her alcoholic, polio-stricken husband could scrounge up from the occasional odd job. She would make a large pot of oatmeal for breakfast, bake it for lunch, and the school-age kids would help neighbors with chores in exchange for their supper. Family lore says that when Eleanor's last son was born, she tried to refuse the baby, and when the doctor placed him on her chest anyway, she flung the newborn across the room. The baby was okay. She, clearly, was not. I cannot fathom the depths of fury and despair that would cause a woman to do that. I suspect Eleanor was trying to protect her daughters by hiring them out as live-in help, but it comes as no surprise to me that she was initially unable to accept my grandma's allegations about the pastor whose family she had been sent to live with. My grandma was the victim, but her mother wasn't exactly swimming in options either.

I have compassion for those who resort to minimization and denial. Some people are just trying to survive. Some are trying to defend a loved one, or struggling to justify what they perceive to be the least-bad option. Others come from such a different world that they truly cannot fathom the truths survivors have revealed to them. It is too much to take in, too threatening to their worldview, too frightening to believe. It is tempting to shrink back when the line advances toward us, keeping our distance instead of confronting it head-on. But if we are going to help adolescent girls by disrupting the cycle of gender-based violence, we are going to have to let go of cherished illusions, shine a light on the monsters lurking under our beds, and be willing to face some really uncomfortable truths.

Hear me, though: If you are personally in danger, or if you are too wounded to fight right now, you are off the hook. If that's the case, my prayer is that a host of God's people will come charging to the rescue and help you get what you need to heal.

But the rest of us? We need to hold the line. We need to stop downplaying abusive behavior, stop making excuses, stop dismissing uncomfortable allegations, and start speaking up when someone crosses the line, or seems to be inching toward it.

But how can we hold the line in a world so ravaged it's hard to perceive where the line even belongs, much less distinguish between the perpetrators we are supposed to be opposing and the victims we are supposed to be helping—who often turn out to be one and the same?

Let's see what the Bible has to say about this.

JAEL FLIPS THE SCRIPT

The Bible, like life, is rife with stories of gender-based violence. Abuse. Enslavement. Rape. Murder. Torture. Kidnappings.

Forced marriages. Exploitation. It is there, in all its horrifying depravity, and the stories hint at realities that are even worse. Realities that untold numbers of women around the world are all too familiar with.

These texts become a stumbling block for many people— those who are unable to reconcile the ugliness of the stories with the beauty of a loving God. Why don't the biblical authors roundly condemn every instance of such behavior? Why do they sometimes seem to approve of it, glory in it, or even on rare occasion, insinuate that it is God's will?

While the Bible is the inspired Word of God, it is important to understand that it shows up dressed in humanity's dirty laundry far more often than most of us would like. Just as Jesus, the ultimate Word of God, took on the constraints of human flesh and limited himself to a place and time in human history during his sojourn on earth, the written Word uses the particularities of language, culture, and context to communicate with human beings in the only way we are capable of understanding. And human language, culture, and context can be ugly, especially when viewed in retrospect.

Could God devise a way to download God's perfect will about every situation directly into our brains? Certainly. Could we withstand it, much less comprehend it, in our current unglorified state? Certainly not. In Exodus 33, God tells Moses that God will cause all his goodness to pass in front of him and proclaim the holy name in his presence. But Moses will have to hide in a rock cleft and only catch a glimpse of God's back, because no one could see God's face and live. Just as we see by the light of the sun, but cannot stare directly into it, God is too much for us without some sort of filter to accommodate our humanity. Since we cannot raise ourselves to

God's level, God meets us where we are, mired in the grit and grime of this world. God is patient with us as we undergo the slow process of transformation that will not be fully realized until Jesus comes again and makes all things new. And so the wisdom of God comes to us wrapped in the words and stories of humanity, and those who have ears, let them hear.

Since stories about gender-based violence are as common as water, in the Scriptures and in our world, it may be interesting to look at a story where the script was flipped. Where the counter-narrative of women won out for once and was a cause for rejoicing. And no one knew how to flip the script like Deborah and Jael.

You may have heard the story. Judges 4:4 leads off with this startling statement: "Now Deborah, a prophet, the wife of Lappidoth, was leading Israel at that time." Wow! The understated way in which the author communicates this suggests that this situation wasn't as shocking as later generations would find it. Indeed, women often have more influence in tribal societies than in nations with a strong central government. But in any case, Deborah was functioning as Israel's spiritual and civic leader, just as Moses had done before her, and Samuel would do after her. A bully named Sisera, who commanded nine hundred iron chariots, had been oppressing God's people for the last twenty years, and Deborah was fed up. She sent for one of Israel's warriors, a man named Barak, and told him to gather an army and engage Sisera on the shores of the Kishon River, near Mount Tabor. Barak said he would only do it if she went with him, and Deborah told him that if he was going to be that way, the glory for this fight would go to a woman.

Enter Jael.

The battle went down just as Deborah had said it would. Barak and Deborah mustered Israel's armies, God went out before them and routed the Canaanites, and Sisera wound up fleeing on foot "to the tent of Jael, the wife of Heber the Kenite, because there was an alliance between Jabin king of Hazor and the family of Heber the Kenite" (Judges 4:17). Jael, apparently, had no such alliance in her own heart.

There is a danger in reading too much into Scripture, ascribing motives to people that are not clearly spelled out. There is also a danger in not reading enough into Scripture— of spending so much time gazing at the dazzling surface that you miss the depths beneath. The undertones of Jael's story writhe with fury, and the sexual innuendo is hard to miss. One has to wonder. Was Jael a victim of Sisera's cruelty? Or perhaps a sister, or a daughter, or a friend of someone who was?

Jael went out to lure the fleeing commander into her tent, enjoined him not to be afraid, and tucked him into her bed. When he asked for water, she gave him a soothing skin of warm milk, and then stood guard at the entrance—until he had fallen asleep. Then Jael took up a hammer, crept over to the bed, and impaled the Canaanite commander with a tent peg. *The Book of Biblical Antiquities*, an ancient source of extra-biblical legends written around the time of Jesus, has Sisera crying out, "I die like a woman!" and Jael telling Sisera, "Go, boast before your father in hell, and tell him you have fallen into the hands of a woman."

Brutal.

In a macabre twist of poetic justice, a lone, vulnerable woman impaled the powerful aggressor in her bed. And the Israelites went wild with joy. The Song of Deborah, immortalized in Judges 5, waxes poetic about Jael's conquest, calling her "most blessed of women" and describing the slaying in gory detail. The song ironically imagines Sisera's mother waiting and worrying at her windowsill, and her handmaidens comforting her with the idea that Sisera must still be dividing the spoils, "a woman or two for each man" (Judges 5:30). But not today, Satan! Jael flipped the script, and it was glorious.

Now, I am not saying that violence should be met with violence or that women should run around impaling rapists with tent pegs. But this is one instance in which the Bible gives us a glimpse into a female revenge fantasy, without moralizing about violence. The female counter-narrative won out, and there is a deeper symbolism to this story that we will look at in just a bit.

But Jael's story isn't the norm, is it? For every woman celebrated for outfoxing a predator, there are countless victims. Jael's story may make us want to cheer, but it is just tit for tat, with the scales falling on the side that looks more like justice for once. And while Jael's actions may have spared some innocent lives, in the end, tit for tat will destroy us all. No, if we're going to address the epidemic of violence in general, and gender-based violence in particular, we can't rely on outraged women wielding weapons. We need something more.

What if, instead of the male narrative or the female narrative, *God's* narrative won out? What would that look like?

JESUS MEETS THE WOMEN OF JERUSALEM

September is usually the best time of year in the Northwoods— warm, with buttery sunlight filtering through leaves that are just beginning to change, and air that smells like apples and campfires and the spicy exhale of drying foliage. But that weekend we'd had storms, and fog so thick you couldn't even see the lake. I didn't mind, cloistered behind the thick stone walls of the monastery I had retreated to for a few days of solitude. But when the sun muscled its way through the fog on Sunday afternoon, I couldn't help myself—I had to go outside and take a walk.

I meandered along the paths between the woods and the cemetery and slowed when I reached the stations of the cross. I had been pondering the slow, brutal, shame-filled process of crucifixion, and the connections it bore to the violence so many women are subjected to. As I walked the stations, those connections became even stronger, Jesus' passion weaving itself together with the stories of women who were heavy on my heart. The desperate pleas for the cup to be removed. The betrayal of a loved one. The friends who couldn't take the heat and scattered to the wind. The legalists intent on ensnaring the victim and condemning them with their own words. That last friend standing who finally distanced himself. Heartbreak after heartbreak, betrayal after betrayal, in the messed-up tableau of tragedy familiar to so many victims.

Finally, there was a bright spot in the stations—a stranger stepping forward to help, shouldering some of the burden that couldn't be borne alone. My shoulders slumped in relief, but the words burned into the next cross made my breath catch in my throat:

"Jesus meets the women of Jerusalem."

It is a scene that has been imagined a thousand different ways, but never without portraying a sense of connection, of soul-deep understanding between Jesus and the women. Once, Jesus had healed their illnesses, banished their demons, and invited them into a beloved community. Now it was their turn to minister to him, in the only way they could.

By refusing to flinch away from his pain or turn their eyes from his suffering. By walking alongside his bruised, beaten body. By stifling their own hysteria so they could be a soothing presence for him. By bearing silent witness to the injustice being done and daring to stand on the side of the doomed, because the side of the doomed was the side of the righteous, and they would die before deserting him.

Jesus had met the women in the depths of their misery—in the darkest, most painful parts of their lives—and he had held his hand out to them instead of flinching away. Now they returned the favor. The crucifixion was Jesus' enthronement, and the handmaidens who attended him were glorious. They knew what it was to suffer, to be scorned and rejected, and they stayed at his side throughout the whole ordeal, midwifing him as his body broke and gave birth to new life.

Jesus met the women of Jerusalem. He meets them still. The question is, Whose side will we chose to stand on: the side of the crucified, or the side of the crucifiers?

KILLING VIOLENCE

What happened at the cross, and what does it tell us about God's response to violence? Without delving too far into different atonement theologies (most of which have some merit), I will say this: while some see the cross as the punitive compromise of a violent God, I believe that God was in fact the victim on the cross, and we were the perpetrators.

Let me say that again. God was the victim. We were the perpetrators.

You may object to the idea that an all-powerful God could be a victim. If so, let me tell you a story. My oldest son has autism. When he was young, there were times when he would spiral into uncontrollable fits, screaming and flailing as he tried to cope with a world that was too much for him. These were especially bad during his toddler years. When he would go into a fit, I used to sit cross-legged on the floor and pull him onto my lap, rock him, and sob. I'd wrap my arms tight around him, pinning him against my body so he couldn't gnash at his precious little arms or bash his head against anything harder than my chest. Sometimes I got scratched. Sometimes I got bruised. And always, always my heart was breaking. It was not my son's fault. He didn't know any better, and he was incapable of doing any better. He was not trying to hurt me. And yet he truly, objectively hurt me.

Now, I could have chosen to stand out of range of my panicking baby. He couldn't have harmed me if I hadn't allowed it. But I loved him, and I knew that any bruises and scratches I might get trying to comfort him and keep him safe were nothing compared to the damage he might inflict on himself if I did not. I willingly allowed myself to be hurt, and I surrendered my adult body to whatever my toddler could throw at it. In fact, I was more than willing—I would have fought my way through pretty much anything to get to my screaming, terrified, helpless baby.

If that is what a human mother is willing to do for her child, imagine the lengths to which God is willing to go. "Jerusalem, Jerusalem," Jesus mourned, "you who kill the prophets and stone those sent to you, how often I have longed to gather your children together, as a hen gathers her chicks under her wings, and you were not willing" (Matthew 23:37).

Jesus wrapped humanity tight in his arms, taking all the sin, and brokenness, and violence we could throw at him on the cross. He allowed death to swallow him whole so he could destroy it from the inside out. Jesus willingly entered into our suffering to do what his helpless children could not. Through his sacrificial death and resurrection, Jesus dealt a fatal head blow to the serpent who has been terrorizing humanity since the beginning, blazing the trail from darkness to light, from bondage to freedom, from death to life, and carrying us out.

Did you catch that bit about the head blow?

Let's circle back to Jael for a moment. At a conference of the organization Christians for Biblical Equality a few years ago, author and advocate J. Lee Grady pointed out that there is a theme in the Old Testament of "women dealing fatal head injuries to the enemy."[10] Jael is the best known, but there is also the "certain woman" of Judges 9 (NRSV) who chucked a millstone at Abimelek's head when he laid siege to the tower she and her townspeople had taken refuge in. And there is the "wise woman" of 2 Samuel 20, who had Sheba's head thrown over the city wall when Joab and his army assembled against them, looking for the scallywag. This theme can be traced all the way back to Genesis 3:15, which scholars refer to as the *protevangelion*, or "first good news"—the first time God mentions his plan to destroys Satan's schemes by sending Jesus. In this first reference to the good news, God tells the serpent, "And I will put enmity between you and the woman, between your offspring and hers; he will crush your head, and you will strike his heel" (Genesis 3:15).

It is fascinating that this foundational promise notes a special enmity between the woman and the serpent, and that contrary to the common beliefs and customs of the day, it is the *woman's* "seed" who will conquer, with nary a mention of the man standing beside her. There is a lot to unpack here, and I don't think biblical scholars have done nearly enough work on it. Statues of a placid, robed virgin putting her foot on a serpent's neck don't cut it. The promise pointed forward to Mary and Jesus, but Mary wasn't the only woman and Jesus wasn't the only offspring being alluded to. In fact, I think a careful reading of oft-overlooked female narratives in the Bible would suggest that just as women are special targets of violence in our broken world, so too they have a special role to play in dismantling violence and bringing about shalom. This life-giving role is not limited to giving birth, and the powers that be are desperate to suppress it.

Perhaps it has to do with vulnerability. Despite the occasional Jael narrative, women cannot win by overpowering people with their physical strength. Perhaps it has to do with sacrificial generosity. Women regularly offer up their bodies to nurture, birth, and sustain new life. Perhaps it has to do with compassion, with the invisible bond connecting women so closely to their loved ones that they feel it in their own body when loved ones are suffering. The only way to destroy violence, once and for all, is to refuse to perpetuate it. In the book of Revelation, the conquering Lion of Judah is revealed to be a slain lamb. The seed of the women crushed the serpent's head not by might, nor by power, but through the life-giving Spirit of a Creator willing to offer himself up for the creation.

A CHRISTIAN RESPONSE TO GENDER-BASED VIOLENCE

Sometimes I wonder how many women have remained in dangerous circumstances because a pastor, or parent, or neighbor, or "friend" lobbed these verses at them:

> Wives, in the same way submit yourself to your own husbands so that, if any of them do not believe the word, they

may be won over without words by the behavior of their wives. . . . For this is the way the holy women of the past who put their hope in God used to adorn themselves. They submitted themselves to their own husbands, like Sarah, who obeyed Abraham and called him her lord. You are her daughters if you do what is right and do not give way to fear. (1 Peter 3:1, 5-6)

I could name off the top of my head several women who have had these verses used as weapons, of sorts, against them. In my experience, pastors are the primary culprits. What a miscarriage of justice, when the shepherds are more concerned with policing the sheep than with protecting them from predators!

In my church, I teach people that they need to ask themselves three questions every time they approach a passage of Scripture. What sort of literature is this? What was the author trying to communicate? And what would it have meant to the original audience? This requires some work, but if we don't do our best to understand the Bible in its social, historical, and literary context, we risk seriously misinterpreting it. The Bible is not a cut-and-dried rulebook for life: it is a collection of narratives, and poems, and histories, and letters, and yes, rulebooks, that tell the story of how God has interacted with humanity over millennia. Oftentimes, the takeaway is not in the specifics of the stories, but in the principles underlying them—the spirit of the law, instead of the letter of the law.

The women Peter was speaking to didn't have many options. They couldn't file for divorce, and if their husbands divorced them, they had no way to support themselves, and risked catastrophic ruin. Compliance was the safest option, and Peter, knowing their circumstances, shored up their courage. But make no mistake: gender-based violence is a sin, and followers of Jesus should do their level best to oppose it, whether that means confronting perpetrators or refusing to enable them by acting as their personal punching bag. People will sin against us; that is inevitable. But we are not doing those people any spiritual favors by allowing them to continue sinning against us if we have another option.

Living as faithful disciples of Jesus in this world means living with a lot of tension, from within and without. Following Christ is not easy, or simple, or clean, and the more you engage with the brokenness around you, the more complicated it becomes. The question of how Christians should respond to violence against themselves, against others, and against the most vulnerable among us is one of those areas of tension. We can, however, address common patterns of thought and behavior that we know are contrary to the way of Christ, and begin there.

One of the most insidious problems in Christianity occurs when those with power encourage those with less power to carry crosses they have no business bearing, typically in a way that benefits the powerful at the expense of the vulnerable. We've been at it for millennia. Wives told to submit to abusive husbands. Enslaved people told to submit to the men who enslaved them. Girls told to forgive and forget instead of pressing charges. Oppressed groups enjoined to be peaceful by the very people who are violating them. It sounds good on the surface—pious, even—and a deep desire to please God can keep sincere people compliant in their suffering. But it is sick. The blame does not lie with the sufferer, but with the powers that impose crosses on the vulnerable in the first place. That is the very definition of antichrist, regardless of whether those powers have appropriated Jesus' name.

We all know that as followers of Jesus we are expected to pick up our crosses and follow him—through suffering, through persecution, and through death, if it comes to that. I am not denying that, and I pray that God keeps me, along with the rest of his flock, faithful through the big and not-so-big trials of this life. But Christians have made two significant mistakes in our approach to addressing violence. We have resorted to violence ourselves, tying heavy loads on other people's shoulders that we ourselves will not move a finger to lift. And we have remained passive in the face of injustice, bowing to power instead of defending the plight of the suffering. Both these approaches make an idol of worldly power, giving it preference over the upside-down kingdom of God.

TREATING THE WOUND AT ITS SOURCE

Here is the problem Christians run into, again and again, when trying to address gender-based violence: we treat the wound but not its source. Maybe it's better than nothing, or maybe it's just perpetuating the problem by giving women the strength to go back and sustain another wound. Yes, we've got to bind up the brokenhearted, but if we're going to make any actual progress, we've got to turn more of our attention to the source of those wounds. And that isn't found on a woman's body; it is found in the festering abscesses of our own souls.

This is the point where I could tell you to support your local women's shelter, or find out what resources your community has in place to help vulnerable runaways. This is the point where I could suggest learning about the signs of trafficking and the tells of abuse, and urge you to consider

becoming a foster parent. This is the point where I could encourage you to buy fair trade gifts from artisans who have
escaped sex trafficking and are trying to rebuild their lives, or
to volunteer for a teen crisis hotline, or to support organizations working to create more just laws around the world, or to
lobby for better enforcement of just laws here at home.

Those are all good ideas, and you should look into them.
The fact that you are holding this book in your hands suggests that you probably have done some of them already. You
already care deeply about the plight of women and girls and
want to help. So pick a course of action and dive in! I will
cheer you on.

But I am not going to spend what remains of this chapter
talking about the thousands of incredible organizations that
exist to help women and girls suffering from gender-based violence. I want to talk about the source of the wound. Because
here is the thing: if you believe God values marriage above a
woman's life, any safety you can offer an abused wife is short-
lived. If you believe God created females for the benefit of
males, your anti-trafficking efforts will simply lead girls into
another form of slavery. If you believe God ordained fathers to
have the final say in their household, what right do you have
to intervene when a father is treating his daughter harshly or
handing her over to someone else who will? If you believe
that females are meant to submit to male leadership and men
are designed to lead women, how can you possibly empower
young women to break free from the chains the men in their
lives have bound them in?

Get mad at me if you want. Wrestle with how my interpretation and application of Scripture compares with your
own. But please, do the wrestling. Grab on to Scripture, grab

on to biblical scholarship, grab on to the stories of women, grab on to God, and refuse to let go until you have a better understanding of God's heart for women and girls. If you've wrestled all night and are still conflicted, give up and grab on to Jesus. Fix your eyes on his face, and gaze deep into his eyes. That should clear things up right quick.

Stopping gender-based violence begins with us. It begins with refusing to perpetuate it in thought, word, or deed. It begins by teaching others to do the same. It begins by calling sin *sin*, by refusing to bow our heads to it, by choosing to live free of it, no matter what the world may say or do to us. It begins by taking a good, hard look at our own relationships—whether we are male or female—and considering the impact we are having and legacy we are leaving: where we are sowing death and where we are sowing life. It begins by rooting out the seeds of violence we are carrying in our own hands and offering them up to God so he can trade them for the seed of Life instead. It begins with dying to sin, violence, and death, and rising to Life.

FIVE

Ready or Not

GIRLS AND EARLY PARTNERING

I remember coming up the stairs at the wedding, wishing I had my keys in a pocket in my dress so I could get in my car and drive away. My brothers were crying."

Julie was fourteen when she began dating an eighteen-year-old from her church. At first it was fun, and they seemed to want similar things in life, right down to the sort of home they dreamed of building. But it didn't take long for Julie to notice that he had a horrible temper. She tried to break it off, but her mother had determined that the young man, who was on a solid career path and planned on staying local, would be a good match for her daughter. "I didn't want to be with him, but my mother said that she wouldn't be able to hold her head up if we broke up," Julie says. "Maybe she thought you could only date one person; maybe she thought we were having sex; I don't know."

Julie did break up with him a couple of times, but then the emotional bombardment would begin. "He'd throw a tantrum and drive off in a rage, and Mom would say 'See? He's going to kill himself, and it's all your fault.'" Julie had it hammered into her head that daughters were to do what they were told, that her own thoughts and feelings were not to be trusted, because her parents knew what was best, that the only option available to her as a good Christian girl was to become a wife and mother—preferably as soon as possible. Her mother threatened to call the pastor and make her go up before the congregation for official church censure when she didn't submit to her parents' demands.

"When you're made to believe that you don't matter, that what you want doesn't matter, you become malleable to abusers," Julie says. "Once, in high school, one of my teachers made everyone write an essay titled 'Who Are You?' All I could think of were my favorite colors, and things I liked. I couldn't speak to my actual identity back then—that I am strong, and faithful, and a child of God. I kept getting Fs on this paper! I'd ask the teacher to provide an example, to explain what she was looking for, and she'd say 'No, you should know who you are.'"

Julie literally flunked identity.

She coped by numbing down her innate sense of danger and self-preservation and doing what was expected of her. "When you're seventeen or eighteen, it's easy to delude yourself that if you just wish hard enough for it to be okay, and pray hard enough for it to be okay, and do everything just right, everything will be okay and he won't blow up. I felt like once the wedding invitations were sent out, that was it. There was no way to get out of it without leaving home. And I was still in high school." Not knowing what else to do, Julie married him a few months after graduation.

Julie's story isn't unique. Variations of it play out all around the world. Girls may be pressured into marriage to comply with social or religious norms, or forced into it for the dowry money it will provide their families. They may move in with a man to escape an abusive home life, or because they don't know how to support themselves on their own. Bride kidnappings, in which a man kidnaps a young woman and forces her into a nonconsensual marriage, are not the relic of the past we wish them to be. And I am sure we all know women who married in haste when they discovered they were pregnant. Sometimes young women just fall in love, and then take that relationship to the next level sooner than is wise.

These relationships do not always end in disaster. In fact, my first exposure to the negative statistics surrounding teen marriage came when concerned friends and relatives lobbed them at me.

A GLIMPSE AT THE NUMBERS

I had fallen hard for a boy at college. We met and married in under a year, when I was nineteen years old and he was twenty-one. I have never regretted it. Twenty-two years later, our marriage is older than either of us were at the time, and we have built a life we love. Every person and every relationship is unique, and statistics, while helpful, don't spell out anyone's destiny.

Still, my relatives were right to be concerned. It's difficult to get up-to-date statistics about the longevity of young marriage, because if you look at, say, how many teen marriages end in divorce within ten years, the data is by definition at least ten years old. When you think about how quickly the world is changing nowadays, that might as well be an eternity. If you look at how many early marriages end in divorce within fifteen or twenty years, you're analyzing the outcomes of a whole different generation—the parents or even grandparents of young people considering marriage today, depending on how long the study lasted. But it's the best we've got, so let's dive in.

A 2002 study from the CDC, which is still widely used in the United States, shows that 48 percent of marriages involving a partner who is under eighteen, and 40 percent of marriages involving an eighteen- or nineteen-year-old, end in divorce within a decade. That's compared to 29 percent for marriages that began between the ages of twenty and twenty-four, and 24 percent for marriages among the twenty-five-and-over set.[1] The divorce rate is going down among millennials, but that is largely because they are cohabiting instead of marrying, and the statistics are even worse for cohabiters. Sixty-eight percent of domestic partnerships that began when one partner was nineteen or younger, and 60 percent of those that began between twenty and twenty-four, were over within a decade. Compare this to 43 percent of those who didn't move in together until they were at least twenty-five.[2]

To sum it up, Americans who marry before twenty-five (which is, perhaps unsurprisingly, the age by which the human brain is fully developed) are about twice as likely to get divorced as those who wait until they have reached the other side of that cognitive teeter-totter, and the younger they are when they marry, the higher the likelihood of divorce. There are other factors, of course. If a young woman can arrange things to make sure she comes from an intact two-parent home, has never been raped, does not suffer from generalized anxiety disorder, and marries a guy who stays employed and is not poor, her chances of staying hitched skyrocket, no matter how old she is when she ties the knot. Bonus points if she is of Asian descent or if either she or her husband go into optometry. Still, barring an affinity for eyeglasses, the easiest way for a woman to stack the marital odds in her favor is to stay out of the game until she is twenty-five.

But don't begin lobbying legislators to raise the marriageable age to twenty-five just yet. It is worth noting that while women around the world are marrying later and less often, they are typically becoming sexually active at about the same age they have been for millennia. In the United States, teenage sexual activity has been decreasing over the past twenty-five years. Still, 13 percent of fifteen-year-old girls, 43 percent of seventeen-year-old girls, and 68 percent of nineteen-year-old women have had sex at least once.[3] It turns out our hormones don't care whether we've finished college; the urges that once drove people toward marriage are simply being fulfilled in less committed contexts.

This creates a whole different set of social and moral issues. Currently, about 40 percent of the babies born in the United States are born to unmarried parents.[4] The lion's share of these children are born to women between the ages of twenty and twenty-four.[5] Sure, marrying before twenty-five leads to a higher likelihood of divorce, but having children out of wedlock leads to a host of undesirable outcomes as well, for everyone involved.

And what about Christians committed to the idea of remaining celibate outside of marriage? A 2009 study showed that a whopping 80 percent of unmarried evangelicals between the ages of eighteen and twenty-nine have had sex—only 8 percent less than the general population.[6] As a pastor and as a parent, I find this deeply troubling. I've already written about the problems inherent in evangelical purity culture—and they are legion—but we can add to those the fact that it doesn't even work. We've created a lot of shame and secrecy and kept our young people more ignorant than they should be about the facts of life. And all our yammering on about purity and modesty and courtship has not prevailed against our permissive culture and the tsunami of post-adolescent biology and actually prevented people from having sex.

Maybe we should have focused on modeling and teaching faithfulness to Jesus instead of faithfulness to some hypothetical future spouse. Idolatry comes in all sorts of forms, after all, and those who were taught to worship future spouses with their virginity can very easily see visions of their god in the first candidate who smiles at them. Being faithful to Jesus, on the other hand, is about much more than how we express our sexuality. It doesn't require less of us—in fact, Jesus-focused teaching calls us to a higher, whole-life standard than moralistic teaching does—but can we just acknowledge for a moment that the goal of authentic Christianity has never been to shape females into good little virgins who become good little wives and mothers? (That was the goal of, oh, pretty much every earthly kingdom since the beginning of time, but never the kingdom of heaven. Look at the lives of the women named in Jesus' genealogy in Matthew 1 if you need proof.) The goal of authentic Christianity has always been for us to surrender our lives so we can be transformed in the image of Christ, no matter our gender, age, or background.

When I hear that 80 percent of unmarried young adults who self-identify as evangelical Christians have had sex, I don't see a morality crisis. I see a deep, disturbing, and frankly terrifying discipleship crisis—a vacuum created by moralism trying to pass itself off as transformation and failing. It is sucking in our young people and spitting out confused, ashamed, nominally religious adults who have the vague sense that their faith isn't strong enough to stand up to the pressures of real life on the other side.

MARRYING TOO YOUNG

I wasn't the first woman in my family to get married in my teens. In fact, it was a family tradition. My parents were nineteen and twenty-one when they got married, as were my paternal grandparents. My grandparents had actually wanted to get married at seventeen and nineteen, but while my grandma's parents were fine with it, my grandpa's mother, who had been forced into marriage herself when she was barely fifteen, would have none of it. Her son's young girlfriend was too sickly, my great-grandma said; rheumatic fever had nearly taken her down, and there were concerns about her heart. She belonged at home with her mother, my great-grandma said. She should finish high school, my great-grandma insisted, even if her own stubborn son had dropped out to work.

Great-Grandma Mabel stuck to her guns, even though she loved my grandma to pieces (perhaps *because* she loved my grandma to pieces), and it didn't make her too popular with her son and future daughter-in-law for a while. In the 1940s, any Wisconsinite under twenty-one needed a parent's consent to marry. Great-Grandma Mabel found the voice she had been denied as a teen bride herself and emphatically did *not* consent.

Nowadays, in the United States, most states set the marriageable age at eighteen, although almost every state allows minors to marry under certain circumstances. Only thirty states spell out a minimum age. In 2001, three ten-year-old girls in Tennessee were married to men aged twenty-four, twenty-five, and thirty-one, and in 2006 an eleven-year-old boy in the same state married a twenty-six-year-old woman.[7] Thankfully, Tennessee has now set a minimum age of seventeen. But one has to wonder what the judges who rubber-stamped those unions were thinking, and whether they are still sitting today.

Globally, somewhere between one in five and one in six teenage girls is married or in a domestic partnership. This is actually down significantly, from one in four who partnered off before age eighteen just a few years ago. About 40 percent of young women in West, Central, and sub-Saharan Africa, 30 percent in South Asia, and 17 percent in the Middle East and North Africa say they were married or in a domestic partnership before their eighteenth birthday.[8]

Interestingly, while great strides have been made in reducing child marriage in those parts of the world, the numbers in the Americas have remained largely untouched. Overall, about a quarter of Latin American girls marry or partner off before they are eighteen, although it varies widely from country to country. Nicaragua, where 41 percent of girls marry before their eighteenth birthday, has the dubious distinction of being among the top twenty countries with the highest rate of child marriage worldwide. The sheer size of Brazil and Mexico means that more teenage brides live in those countries than almost anywhere else in the world.[9] Colombia is right up there too. Yet little progress has been made, despite lawmakers' efforts.

Teenage relationships are complicated, and figuring out how to respond to them is complicated as well. UNICEF has declared marriage under eighteen to be a violation of human rights, and if a line must be drawn, that doesn't seem like a bad place to draw it. Twenty-one used to be the age of consent in many places, and that is even better from the standpoint of physical and emotional development. Still, every individual is different, and it is all too easy to judge other people's choices through our own cultural biases or personal experiences.

Personally, I think it makes sense to ask three questions when considering whether a young woman is ready for marriage: Is she legally old enough to make her own decisions, and does she have the freedom to truly consent to or refuse marriage? Has she had the opportunity to acquire the education and skills she needs to thrive in her community? And is she physically developed enough to bear children safely?

Sure, even if all these questions can be answered in the affirmative, a young woman may *still* be better off waiting. But for most young women in modern society, those three questions would put the minimum age for marriage somewhere between eighteen and twenty-two. If unjust laws, abuse, or poverty are systemically preventing young women in any given community from attaining the first two objectives, then focusing on what can be done to solve those problems may be a better starting point than trying to convince girls with few other prospects to delay marriage.

MARRYING TOO LATE?

"My grandma asked me if I have considered in vitro fertilization."

I was sitting on my friend's kitchen floor, being regaled with The Further Tales of Family Members Trying to Fix Her Life. They had always done it but had amped it up after she turned thirty. Her irascible grandma was particularly intent on getting her set up with an eligible bachelor or, failing that, at least getting her some of his sperm. We couldn't help laughing, but I knew my friend found conversations about her singleness exhausting.

No discussion about the age of marriage would be complete without someone bringing up how today's Peter Pan slackers are letting the biological clock tick-tock away, especially compared to the young age at which people *used* to get married. The idea that people are marrying later in life than they used to is true, to some extent. But how true it is or isn't depends largely on where a person comes from, and whether you measure "early" or "late" from the perspective of age or lifespan.

In the ancient world, and in many traditional cultures up to this day, it was common for women to get married shortly after menarche, the onset of menstruation. However, while women in the past entered puberty at about the same age we do, between ten and twelve, they typically began menstruating significantly later, thanks to a variety of environmental factors including malnutrition and disease.[10] In fact, while most girls nowadays begin their period around age twelve, fourteen was closer to the norm for most of human history, and sixteen or seventeen wasn't unusual, especially for the overworked, underfed peasant class. In the United States, in

1900, the average girl started her period at 14.7 years old.[11] In 1928 it was 13.9, in the 1950s it was 13.5, by the 1970s it was 12.8, and now it is 12.5.[12] So even in cultures where girls married very young, they were likely closer to fourteen or fifteen than the twelve or thirteen we would imagine. Those extra two years of physical and emotional development make a big difference.

I read *Romeo and Juliet* for the first time in seventh grade, and I still remember how shocked the entire advanced lit class was when we learned that Juliet was thirteen—the same age we were! Not only that, but Paris, trying to convince Juliet's father to let him woo her, said, "Younger than she are happy mothers made." The teacher had to stop and explain to us that it was common for people to get married in their early teens back then. People died young, so they had to get cracking!

The only problem? My teacher was wrong. In Elizabethan England, girls could marry at twelve and boys at fourteen with their parents' permission, but the actual age of consent was twenty-one, and the mean age of marriage was twenty-seven.[13] In other words, Elizabethans married at about the same age as American Gen Xers! Children from wealthy families were sometimes promised or married off early to cement alliances, but eighteen-year-old Shakespeare would have been considered very young indeed when he married twenty-six-year-old Anne Hathaway.

My grandma used to tell me that in her day, girls who weren't engaged within a year or so of graduating from high school were in danger of being written off as "old maids." The average age of marriage was unusually low in the 1950s, 1960s, and 1970s, with men marrying at twenty-two or twenty-three and women at twenty. In 1900, women were getting married at about twenty-two, and men at twenty-six. In 2000, those numbers had climbed to twenty-five and twenty-six, and now women are marrying—when they do marry—at twenty-seven and men at twenty-nine.[14]

What does this tell us? It tells us that perhaps, in the words of Shakespeare, we're making much ado about nothing. People are still partnering off within the same ten-year window that they always have—or fifteen years, if you take the lower and upper extremes of the age range into account. It's like we're heeding the ticking of a biological alarm clock or something. Moved in with your man and his family at sixteen? Congratulations, you're a Roman noblewoman. Married in your late teens or early twenties? Congratulations, you're your grandma. Tied the knot in your mid- to late twenties? Congratulations, you're an Elizabethan who outsmarted Juliet. Married in your thirties? Congratulations. Seriously, congratulations.

Still, there is no question that partnering off too early can result in dire physical, emotional, social, and economic consequences. There is also the fact that many young women are manipulated into regrettable relationships, cornered into economic dependence, or flat-out forced into marriages without their consent.

So what are we to think about all this? How young is too young to get married? And in a world where different cultures, traditions, socioeconomic issues, and biological considerations weave a tangled web for young women to navigate, who gets to decide? How can we best help young women flourish, both individually and in the context of their family and community?

We could begin by helping young women unhitch their identity and sense of worth from their relationships with other humans. We could usher them toward finding their identity in the fact that they were created in the image of God, and that they are loved by God no matter what.

FALLEN IDOLS

Once upon a time there was a princess who fell in love with a shepherd boy. Her father sent the boy off on an impossible quest, hoping to be rid of the interloping peasant. But the shepherd boy returned with double the bride price, and claimed the princess—and eventually the kingdom—as his own.

It sounds like the perfect setup for a happily ever after, doesn't it? But in reality, David brought little but grief to his first wife, Michal, the daughter of King Saul.

In the whole Hebrew Bible, Michal is the only woman said to love a man. Women's feelings for the men they were married off to seem not to have been of paramount importance in that day and age. Yet the author of 1 Samuel notes that long before the marriage arrangements were made, young Michal was head over heels for David—not unlike her brother Jonathan and most of the populace of Israel and Judah. There is no mention of David loving her in return—a telling omission—but 1 Samuel 18 (NRSV) notes that he was "well pleased to become the king's son-in-law."

Michal is often maligned for taking her husband to task for his half-clothed capering before the ark of the covenant in 2 Samuel 6. But the criticism she receives from preachers, podcasters, and women's Bible study leaders on this point betrays a stunning lack of empathy. I don't think many of us could blame Michal for "despising [David] in her heart" by that point, if we put ourselves in her high-class sandals. Think about it. You develop a crush on your big brother's dreamy best friend—the popular, handsome young man who spends half his time dominating on the battlefield and the other half playing songs he wrote on his lyre. Your father uses your affections to try to get the boy killed, and the boy takes advantage of the opportunity to embed himself more deeply into the royal family. When you discover your father's murderous plot, you risk your own life helping your husband escape, lowering him out your bedroom window and arranging an idol in the bed to make it look like he is still there, buying him time. But he doesn't take you with him, or make arrangements for you to join him, or even intervene when your father marries you off to another man—one who, incidentally, actually seems to care about you and want to be with you.

Then, by the time your first husband returns and demands you back years later, citing the bloody bride price of the two hundred Philistine foreskins he paid for you, he has collected a harem of other wives and concubines, your father and brother are dead, and you have grown old and wise enough to understand that if this man is going to take the throne, he is going to have to do what all new kings do and eliminate the competition—your remaining brothers and nephews, including your sister's children, whom you raised as your own. You yourself are a chess piece strengthening his claim to the throne, but he is unlikely to have children with you, since they would be seen as part of your father's dynasty, not his own.

Michal was right on all counts. David may have been a man after God's own heart, but his relationships with women were, for the most part, spectacular, self-absorbed failures.

The other women may have expected that from the start, and may have even hitched themselves willingly to David's rising star. But Michal—Michal had fallen in love with a ruddy-cheeked shepherd boy who played the lyre and wrote love songs to God, only to find herself married to a savvy politician who had a hand in slaughtering her family. Personally, I think Michal should be congratulated for having the forbearance to not go all Jael on David and murder him in his sleep.

Michal isn't the only woman who has lived to regret marrying her childhood crush. Sometimes it works out beautifully, but young love tends to be long on excitement and short on sense, focused on how one feels in the moment instead of asking what life with this person will be like ten, twenty, thirty, or fifty years down the road. Of course, anyone can marry the wrong person, or marry for the wrong reasons, or lack the maturity to develop a healthy long-term relationship. But the young are particularly vulnerable. They often lack a solid idea of what they want or need, in a partner and in life, until they find themselves locked in a relationship with someone who is incompatible with their values or unconcerned about their flourishing. Michal loved David, but her proximity to her father's rival put her at enormous personal risk. I also don't think concubines and other wives figured into her dreams about her future with her heroic shepherd boy.

Michal is also similar to young women around the world in the fact that, ultimately, she had no choice in the matter. She was happy to marry David—and many people who grew up with the expectation that their marriage would be arranged by others are nonetheless happy to marry the person chosen for them—but no one was looking out for her best interests. She was being used, by both her father and her husband, to acquire something they wanted. The patriarchal culture she lived in had reduced her to a form of currency. She was bought and sold, discarded and taken up again—like a prize horse, or a used car, or a timeshare in Orlando that you don't really want anymore but can't get rid of. Like billions of women throughout history, Michal was treated as if her value resided not in who she was, and whose image she was created to bear, but in the benefit she brought to the men in her life—first her father, and later her husband and the children he intentionally denied her.

TACKLING TRADITION

"Women in Kenya will not be treated as equals until we do away with the dowry system."

The room erupted in shocked chatter, but the woman plowed ahead, a queenly figurehead cutting straight through the choppy tide of culture. How could women be equal, she asked, when they were traded for cows? When women themselves measured one another's worth by the size of the dowry given for them? When parents felt entitled to take their daughters back if the dowry had been too paltry, and husbands held the price they had paid over their wife's head as proof that she owed him?

We had covered a variety of touchy topics over the course of the conference, from bride kidnappings to creation order to menstruating female priests presiding over communion. But none of them drew the response that this woman's assault on the dowry system did. It was tradition, the way marriages had always been arranged. It was meant to protect the woman— how else could a man prove he could provide for her? What would it do to women's self-esteem if men stopped paying dowries? Wouldn't they feel that their husbands didn't value them? One older man, trying to be diplomatic, suggested that perhaps the dowry could be given to the couple themselves instead of to the woman's father and uncles, to help them get a good start in life. This was slightly less scandalous, but people still struggled to see how it could work.

At lunchtime, a young Anglican priest who himself was saving up a bride price asked what my husband had done about a dowry. He was shocked to learn that dowries weren't a thing in my culture. Hadn't we read Genesis? What did we do about Abraham, who sent his servant off to choose a bride for his son Isaac with ten camels loaded down with good things for her family (Genesis 24)? Did I actually mean that my husband had gotten me without paying *anything*?

Yes, I said—although if I'm honest, that was only half true. My husband had bought me two rings, one containing a diamond. While modest by American standards—the amount a broke college student could save up for—the money spent on those rings probably could have financed a respectable dowry in western Kenya.

And the rings were the least of it. My in-laws had forked out hundreds of dollars to put on a rehearsal dinner. My dad had sold his motorcycles to buy the satin dress in which I walked down the aisle, and my parents had taken out a second mortgage to cover the rest of it—the food, the flowers, the cake, the embossed invitations. Being nineteen and in love, I gave very little thought to any of this—aside from which cake to choose and what color I wanted the flowers to be. It was tradition.

I'm not trying to be all Ebenezer Scrooge about wedding celebrations, but I am trying to point out that we Westerners have no reason to be smug. I mean, I'm from Wisconsin. Cows are much more practical than golden rings, and if I had sunk all the money spent on my wedding into cattle, I could have had a respectable starter herd, even in the United States.

The magnificent dissenter at the conference was right: the dowry system commodifies women and incentivizes their families to marry them off, regardless of whether it is in the woman's best interest. But at least in the Kenyan system the money stays in the family and provides life-giving nourishment. Did you ever see the old Looney Toons cartoon in which a wealthy old woman in a rocking chair calmly throws bundles of cash into the fire? Western wedding traditions have a dark underbelly of their own, but most of us never think to question it. When it comes to love and marriage, we don't want ethics or sense messing with The Way Things Have Always Been Done.

Nevertheless, we can't talk about early partnering without talking about money. Some people pair off for love, and some for religious or cultural reasons. But by and large, when unhappy brides marry too young, economics are involved. Perhaps the dowry money will pay for her father's antiretroviral treatment, or help her mother start a business, or keep her brothers in school, or get her family out of the refugee camp and into an apartment. Perhaps her parents can't afford to care for her, and marrying her off to a man with decent prospects truly does seem like the best way to ensure their beloved daughter's future. Maybe a young woman rushes into a relationship because she has no idea how to take care of herself, and taking shelter under someone else's wing seems like the safest bet. Of course there are people who simply see an opportunity to turn a profit on their young, female relatives and take it, but life is seldom that cut-and-dried. Most parents really do love their daughters and want good things for them. The question is what our societies have conditioned us to think of as good for young women—and whether their families have the means to provide it.

Education is the best barrier against early marriage. Statistically, even seven years of education means girls marry four years later and have two fewer children.[15] Education gives young women options, stretches their imagination about what they could become, and gives them a way to provide for themselves. If they do marry, they can marry because they want to, not because they are economically dependent. There are many ways to help girls get a solid educational start; in fact, now might be a decent time to flip back to chapter 2 and refresh your memory. Pay special attention to strategies—like providing boarding school fees, bicycles, and feminine hygiene products—that help teenage girls stay in school.

Unfortunately, not all girls can afford to attend school, and even when they do, it is often a drain on their family's finances. This puts girls at risk of being partnered off early to ease the economic burden on their family, to access the dowry money a man is willing to pay for them, or to provide for the girls themselves if no one else is able to do so. This is where female-focused economic development comes in handy. Study after study has shown that the best way to improve outcomes for children is to empower their mother, socially, politically, and economically. Remember my great-grandma Mabel, and how that once-upon-a-time fifteen-year-old bride delayed my grandparents' marriage by two years? Women who have the means to fight for their daughters—and daughters-in-law— as well as the vision to see a better future for them, often will.

Barring that, one of the best ways to avoid economically motivated early marriages is to empower the girl herself and help her family see the girl as an asset (aside from the dowry she could draw) instead of a liability. There are many organizations that help women of all ages learn a trade, start small businesses, manage livestock, or leverage their interests and investments. Look deeper than the pictures of children and chickens on the front page of their catalogs: World Vision and Heifer International both have programs focused on economically empowering women, and the microfinance organization Kiva has always been quite female-focused. Thousands of smaller organizations focus on a variety of projects in locations all over the world. Do you have a passion for beekeeping, or soap making, or sustainable farming? Are you into business development or economic investment or STEM training for girls? Do you care deeply about young women in Honduras, or Nepal, or your own backyard? Do a little research, find an organization you can get passionate about, and dive in. If it's a grassroots organization run by people from the community themselves, that's even better.

And of course, one of the best ways to prevent young women from falling headlong into regrettable relationships is to make sure they can stand on their own two feet—not only economically but spiritually and emotionally as well. Help them sink their roots down deep into Jesus and his love. That way, when the winds and the rains and the droughts come, they are established and firm. That way they become oaks of righteousness, stretching strong branches toward heaven, instead of clinging vines desperate for something to support them, no matter the shape into which it bends them.

SIX

Babies Having Babies

GIRLS AND EARLY CHILDBEARING

My mother pulled me out of the tribal school in fourth grade because I had this idea I was going to have a kid in high school." The young woman sitting next to me on the airplane tucked her legs up into her chest, resting her heels on the seat to stretch. We had been sitting on the tarmac for nearly an hour, waiting for the congestion at O'Hare to clear, and our conversation had wound its way from art to economics to community health. "Everyone had a kid in high school," she said. "At the end-of-the-year ceremony, they'd line up all the girls who were pregnant and the community would present them with a gift basket. I wanted a gift basket!"

Children are always a gift. The young woman's community had the right idea, affirming the ongoing life of a community that has been subject to centuries of direct and indirect genocide. They didn't only offer gift baskets, affirmation about the goodness of new life, and emotional support; the tribe runs a robust community health program focused on the needs of mothers and children as well.

But when the gift of children is received by people who have not developed the strength and maturity to carry it well, that gift can become burdensome. The young woman's mother knew that, and she made a difficult decision she hoped would safeguard her own child's future. It seems to have worked: the girl whose goal was to be presented a gift basket and all the good things that came with it went to college and now works for the tribe, reinvesting into the life of her community the education and opportunities she accessed. She herself is a gift.

Childbearing has always been dangerous, especially for the young. In fact, complications of pregnancy and childbirth are the leading cause of death for girls between the ages of fifteen and nineteen worldwide.[1] Let that sink in for a moment. A teenage girl is more likely to die from childbirth, pregnancy-related diseases, or a botched abortion than she is to die from an illness or accident.

Part of the problem is that while most teenage bodies are capable of pregnancy, they are truly not ready for it yet. The body does not transition from child to woman overnight, and the onset of menstruation typically occurs years before a girl is full grown, with a physiology that allows her to safely carry and give birth to a baby. While everyone's body is unique, the numbers show this loud and clear. Girls who give birth between fifteen and nineteen are twice as likely to die in childbirth as women in their twenties, and their babies are 50 percent more likely to die as well. Girls who are fourteen or younger are five times more likely to die than women in their twenties.[2]

In 2018, Dr. Denis Mukwege was awarded a Nobel Peace Prize for his work treating obstetric fistulas in the Democratic Republic of the Congo. Obstetric fistulas occur when trauma to the pelvic area damages the tissues, and they can cause incontinence, nerve damage, infection, and death. They can be the result of a particularly violent rape, like the cases Dr. Mukwege is famous for treating, but typically, obstructed labor is the culprit. Teenage girls are especially susceptible to fistulas. Given that the average girl begins menstruating at twelve, many thirteen-year-old girls could probably conceive; but would you assume that their pelvises could accommodate a baby's head?

Some young teens can give birth with no problems, but it is an impossibility for many others. Without medical intervention, there is little hope for them or their babies. In *Half the Sky*, Nicholas Kristof and Sheryl WuDunn tell the story of Mahabouba, a young Ethiopian woman who was sold into marriage at thirteen and escaped, pregnant, at fourteen. She couldn't afford a birth attendant, so she labored alone, in a hut near her uncle's house, for seven days. Finally someone called for help, but the baby was dead, and Mahabouba was incontinent and unable to walk. She was abandoned to die. Miraculously, she managed to drag herself to a nearby village and to the home of a missionary, who took her to a fistula hospital.

Everyone should have access to good maternal healthcare, but it is particularly crucial for teenage girls. A skilled practitioner, who can monitor a young woman's health and perform a C-section if necessary, can mean the difference between life and death for mother and child. Unfortunately, only 47 percent of women in impoverished countries have a doctor, nurse, or midwife attending their deliveries.[3]

It's not all doom and gloom. Maternal health has made huge strides in recent decades. According to the World Health Organization, maternal mortality dropped by 50 percent between 1990 and 2013. That's an amazing achievement! All the work that countries, health systems, and nonprofits have been doing to advance maternal health is paying off. This focus on the well-being of mothers and babies has not always existed, and is nothing to take for granted.

Childbearing is surprisingly political. For instance, during World War I, more American women died in childbirth than American men died on the battlefield. Losing that many young women was just the norm, and few people stopped to question whether anything could be done about it—at least, few people in power did. Once women got the vote, infant mortality dropped by 16 percent and maternal mortality dropped by 12 percent almost overnight, thanks in large part to the passage of the Sheppard-Towner Act, officially known as the Promotion of the Welfare and Hygiene of Maternity and Infancy Act. By the time the first wave of Sheppard-Towner babies were having babies of their own, they were 70 percent less likely to die in childbirth than their grandmothers.[4] Reducing infant and maternal mortality is all about access to healthcare, and access to healthcare is all about public policy, something we will touch on later in this chapter.

RISING STAKES

"I should have given him up for adoption."

I scraped my jaw up off the floor, schooled my features, and gave the woman sitting next to me my full attention. She was gazing at her elementary-age son, who was playing in the next room. "My parents, my pastor—they all told me I didn't need to get married. That I could choose a great family who wanted a child, give the baby up for adoption, and move on with my life. I wonder how things might have been different if I had."

I've known a lot of teen moms who resented being advised to give their babies up, and others who affirmed choosing adoption. But this was the first time I had ever heard a woman say she regretted *not* having given a child up for adoption. She loved her child—loved him deeply—but neither of their lives had been easy. Somehow, she conjured the courage to be honest about the what ifs that plagued her as she considered her life, and her child's.

Girls with access to modern medicine face fewer physical dangers than they would have one hundred years ago, but the social and economic toll of teen pregnancy is higher than ever. Maybe not directly—in the Global North, at least, girls are unlikely to have a scarlet letter pinned to their chest if they get pregnant out of wedlock. But the gap between survival and flourishing has widened exponentially, and navigating that gap with a baby on your back is no easy task.

My great-grandma Mabel was an orphan. Her father had disappeared into the wild, wild West (he was later discovered bartending in the Sunshine State), and her beautiful young mother had died, ostensibly of a broken heart. She lived with her grandparents until her grandmother died and her grandfather's new wife wanted her out. The options available to her were marriage or a children's home. Fifteen-year-old Mabel took the safest route available to her, and married a shy but steadfast cousin she knew would be kind to her. She was sixteen when she gave birth to the first of their fourteen children, my great-uncle George.

While my great-grandma would have preferred to delay marriage, stay in school, and have more opportunities to explore, she wasn't too far out of step with the community around her. Like most women of her day, she relied more heavily on her ability to grow food, run a household, and mend people and things than she did on her eighth-grade education—although her neighbors did think it odd that she would stop whatever she was doing to read when a child came to her with a book. They were as poor as church mice, and her life was hard, but it was hard in the same way everyone else's life was hard. In 1922, there was nothing exceptional about leaving school and having a child at sixteen.

Nowadays, that is not the case. We live in an increasingly complex world, and the skills required to thrive in it are not what they were one hundred years ago. It is not uncommon for women who have children when they are young to spend the rest of their lives playing catch-up, struggling to make up for the skills and connections other young women were developing while they were navigating the morass of motherhood. Some of them defy the odds, fight through the barriers, and build a healthy life for themselves and their children. Others get sucked further down into the whirlpool of poverty, unable to escape the cycle. And make no mistake: the well-being of mothers is inexorably linked to the well-being of their children. As the mothers go, so go the children. As the children go, so go our communities, and so go our collective futures.

We need to do better for the mothers and children in our midst—especially when the mothers are children themselves.

A CONSPIRACY OF WOMEN

A conspiracy of women: that is what saved Israel. It happened more than once, but never more obviously than in the opening scenes of one of the greatest epics ever told, the exodus. Principled midwives. A desperate mother. An indomitable little girl, and a shrewd noblewoman. Long before Moses encountered the God of his fathers in the burning bush, the God of his mothers was breathing wisdom and courage into the women who would defy the powers to save his life.

As a child, I thought it sounded like a fairy tale, and I interpreted it as such—a true fairy tale. The mother was a shadowy figure who faded away after the prologue, because full-grown fairy-tale women are always dead, evil, or not worth mentioning. The dark-haired girl crouching in the reeds was simply a warm-climate version of Gretel, crouching beside the witch's oven. Pharaoh's daughter was a gasping, wide-eyed anime princess with all the depth and intellect of, well, a gasping, wide-eyed anime princess.

It wasn't until I had become one of those full-grown women whom fairy tales are so uncomfortable with that I realized how wrong I was. Shiphrah, Puah, Jochebed, Miriam—these determined women are the foci of the resistance movement that opens the book of Exodus, and the unnamed Egyptian woman who supports their scheme is no fool either. This is the seed from which the exodus sprang, the act of resistance that sparked the revolution. Moses led the people out, but these women struck the match and started the slow burn to liberation.

It started with saving one little boy and ended with saving a whole people. The individual and the collective, tied up together, as always.

The women of Exodus weren't unique in their salvific contribution to Israel's line. In an essay titled "Mother in Israel," J. Cheryl Exum points out that "while the important events in Israelite tradition are experienced by men, they are often set in motion and determined by women."[5] This is particularly evident in the stories of the matriarchs, and it is fascinating to consider the role they played in protecting and preserving the messianic line—often in direct opposition to their husbands. Father Abraham had many sons, but it was Sarah's son who inherited the promise. While the story is tragic, God told Abraham to submit to Sarah's insistence that he send Hagar and Ishmael away. God had told Rebecca which of her sons was supposed to carry the covenant, and she lied, cheated, and manipulated to make sure Jacob got the blessing that Isaac was determined to give the wrong son. It was the unloved Leah who gave birth to Judah and gave all praise to God, while her sister Rachel's womb was still closed.

Judah's story—or perhaps we should say Tamar's story—is an interesting one. Judah arranged for a young woman named Tamar to marry his firstborn, Er, but Er "was wicked in the Lord's sight; so the Lord put him to death" (Genesis 38:7). Judah instructed his second son, Onan, to sleep with Tamar and get her pregnant, in accordance with the custom of the day. This son would inherit the firstborn's property and care for Tamar once he was grown. Onan realized that if Tamar didn't get pregnant, the firstborn's portion would pass to him, instead of the nonexistent child, once his father died. This seemed preferable, so while he willingly had sex with Tamar, he pulled out to avoid causing pregnancy. God wasn't impressed, and Onan died too. Judah was beginning to catch on to the fact that God wasn't messing around with people who messed around with Tamar, so instead of marrying her to his third son, Shelah, he told her to go home to her father until the boy was older—although Judah had no intention that the match would ever come to be.

When Tamar realized she had been conned, she took action. She traded her widow's weeds for a prostitute's garment, veiled her face, and staked out a spot along the road where she knew her father-in-law would pass. The Bible doesn't comment on why Tamar was so sure this harebrained scheme would work, but I think her confidence gives us a hint about Judah's conflicted character at that point in time. Sure enough, Judah propositioned her, and Tamar slept with him in exchange for his seal, cord, and walking stick—the ancient equivalent of his driver's license and car title. These were supposed to act as security for the goat Judah promised to pay Tamar, but Tamar absconded with them—and the babies newly implanted in her womb—before the goat could be delivered.

This story sounds outrageous to modern ears, and it's easy to consider Tamar's actions trampy. That's because it is almost impossible for us to understand how significant children were in that day and age from a social, financial, and even religious perspective. The early Hebrew concept of an afterlife was murky, and eternal life was something you attained by passing a bit of yourself on in your children. Heirs secured the land and property of families, safeguarding the well-being of the entire clan and everyone who looked to them for support. That's why Onan's actions were so outrageous—he was effectively scrubbing his big brother's name from history and stealing his inheritance while disgracing Tamar and robbing her of a future.

Then there was the added weight of the covenant promise God had made with Abraham's line. Judah's first two sons were dead, and his remaining son was promised to Tamar, but Judah would not allow him to marry her. Judah's line was in danger. Fifteen hundred years before the coming of Christ, Tamar perceived the threat, and acted to secure the messianic line, just as Sarah and Rebecca had done before her. While it sounds crazy to us, there was nothing promiscuous about Tamar's actions in that day and age. She was owed a child, someone in Judah's line was required to give it to her, and she acted in the best interests of everyone involved—and, incidentally, in the best interests of all human history.

Tamar returned to her father's home after the tryst, put her widow's clothing back on, and waited. When three months had passed, Judah was informed that his daughter-in-law had engaged in prostitution and turned up pregnant. Seizing his chance to rid himself and his family of the troublesome woman once and for all, he ordered that she be dragged out and burned alive. Nice, huh? But Tamar had planned for this contingency. When the people came to her father's house to execute her, she gave them Judah's seal, cord, and staff, and told them to take them to her father-in-law and tell him that the owner of those items was the one who had gotten her pregnant.

Tamar: 3; Judah: 0.

This revelation knocked some sense into Judah. He broke down and admitted that Tamar was more righteous than he; that this had all happened because he had shirked his duty by refusing to marry her to Shelah. Judah did the right thing by Tamar, caring for her and the twins she bore as a father would, and not engaging in a sexual relationship with her.

Tamar's courageous actions, and the humility they instilled in Judah, also changed Judah's relationships with other people for the better, as we see when he is reunited with his half-brother Joseph later in the book. And of course Perez, the oldest of Tamar and Judah's twin sons, continued the messianic line. He shows up in the genealogy of Jesus, right there at the very beginning of Matthew's gospel.

One of the fascinating things about this story is the way it highlights the interplay of risk and responsibility in male-female relationships in general, and childbearing in particular. Er and Onan reaped the consequences of their own wicked behavior, but their father considered Tamar liable for their downfall. Judah was perfectly happy to hire the services of a prostitute, but when he found out his daughter-in-law was pregnant, he wanted her burned alive. Other aspects of this story seem downright bizarre to modern readers, but this part is eerily familiar. It is not too difficult for men to hide their sexual indiscretions, but hiding a pregnancy is next to impossible. It takes both a male and a female to make a baby, but without proof of paternity, women have few ways of compelling fathers to take responsibility. Children are a blessing, but the burden of that blessing—a burden meant to be shouldered by two eager, loving parties—is often shoved entirely onto the shoulders of the woman. The rewards of bearing children are high, but so are the risks and responsibilities, especially for females.

WHAT TO DO? TEEN PREGNANCY, CONTRACEPTION, AND ABORTION

"Women can now give up contraceptive methods." John Magufuli, the famously outspoken president of Tanzania, drew international attention when he launched into a rant about birth control at a public rally. "Those going for family planning are lazy. . . . They do not want to work hard to feed a large family and that is why they opt for birth controls and end up with one or two children only."[6]

In fairness to Magufuli, he lives what he speaks. A devout Catholic from humble beginnings, the former teacher and father of five has slashed government spending (including most of his own salary) and used it to fund education and health-care initiatives like the ones he was touting in his speech—the widespread construction of new maternal health centers and district hospitals that would make childbirth safer. His efforts are laudable. But would Tanzania become a healthier place if people followed his advice?

Magufuli's arguments aren't dissimilar to what you often hear in the West, aside from the suggestion that people have a lot of kids (although certain sects in the West promote that too). While the vast majority of sexually active women in the United States have used contraception at some point in their lives, it remains startlingly controversial. Who should use it? Who should pay for it? Which methods should be accessible? And who gets to decide? Parents, partners, the government, insurance companies, employers providing insurance? Even though pregnancy inevitably involves a male and a female, the biological, social, and economic responsibility for managing fertility generally falls on the woman's shoulders—as does the shame if she does not manage it in a way society approves of. Consider Magufuli's comment about *women* giving up contraceptive methods. Where do men fit into this? And how can we all do a better job of supporting young women, regardless of whether they get pregnant?

THE PERSONAL, THE POLITICAL, AND THE POLICING OF FEMALE SEXUALITY

I am pro-life. I was twelve when I learned there was such a thing as abortion, and the very thought made me physically ill, grieving the immensity of the loss. My horror was soon translated into bright, oversized T-shirts proclaiming that "abortion stops a beating heart," and a tiny-feet stickpin given pride of place on my stonewashed jean jacket. My intensity may have been because of the grief I was carrying over my mother's miscarriages. We had just moved from Liberia to the United States, I felt sad and utterly alone, and I daydreamed about the four siblings I knew to be missing from my life, assigning them genders, names, and personalities. I remembered going to a doctor's appointment with my mother and hearing the heartbeat of a baby who would never come home. The thought that anyone would end a pregnancy on purpose was too much to comprehend.

As I got older, however, I grew uneasy about how this played out in American society. It was concerning to me that one political party seemed to have the monopoly on the pro-life vote, limiting single-issue voters' voice in public policy. I was shocked to learn that many insurance policies didn't cover contraception. Didn't pregnancies cost more than the pill? I'd hear people sneer about "welfare queens," and I'd wonder how that connected to the pro-life promise to love and care for single mothers and their babies. Or did that promise only apply to well-groomed white girls from middle-class households who were deemed to be suitably penitent?

But it wasn't until several Christian-owned businesses and nonprofits went to war with the recently passed Affordable Care Act, challenging the new mandate that health insurance was required to include contraception, that I became disillusioned enough to acknowledge that my pro-choice friends had been right about one thing: for many people, the debate seemed to have more to do with policing female sexuality than saving babies. Because if saving babies was the top priority, many outspoken pro-life individuals and organizations were going about it in the entirely wrong way.

Conversations about contraception, abortion, and unplanned pregnancies are fraught with emotion. This is appropriate, given the impact all three have on human lives. It's nothing to take lightly. Unfortunately, however, the fear, shame, and anger surrounding these topics can make it difficult to get a clear-eyed view of the impact they are having on individuals and societies, and it is not unusual for facts to get skewed, because of ignorance or agendas. So let's take a look at the numbers and see what they can tell us. We'll start with a general overview, and then focus on the impact on adolescent girls.

CONTRACEPTIVE USE

Worldwide, about 63 percent of women who are in a committed relationship and are of childbearing age use some form of contraception. These numbers are highest in the Americas, followed by Europe, Asia, and Oceania. The use of contraceptives has increased in Africa, but it still lags far behind the others: while contraceptive use is at 54 percent and 65 percent in northern Africa and southern Africa, respectively, use in western Africa is only 20 percent, use in central Africa, 23 percent, and in eastern Africa, 43 percent. Conversely, eastern Asia has the highest level of contraception use in the world, largely because 83 percent of women of childbearing age in China use contraceptives.[7]

In the United States, 62 percent of women of childbearing age are using contraceptives at any given time, including 90 percent of women who are trying to avoid a pregnancy.[8] Christian religious affiliation does not seem to affect those numbers: 89 percent of sexually active Catholic women and 90 percent of Protestant women who aren't trying to get pregnant use some form of contraception, and 99 percent of both groups report having used it at some point.[9]

Still, some people object to the use of contraception on religious grounds. The arguments can be divided into two broad categories: the belief that contraception short-circuits God's will for human families, and the concern that certain forms of contraception could cause a miscarriage.

The first opinion is an open-and-shut case: if that is what one believes, that is what one believes. The second argument, however, is largely based on the idea that some forms of contraception could have an abortifacient effect, making it difficult for a zygote to implant if conception does occur. IUDs and the morning-after pill have a particularly bad rap in this area.

While modern IUDs are among the most effective forms of contraception available, they still haven't lived down the problems their predecessors caused in the 1970s. IUDs are not, as many people have claimed, abortifacients—they are actually glorified spermicides, preventing fertilization by blocking or destroying sperm (or both), depending on the type of IUD. Plan B, also known as the "morning-after pill," is a victim of its name: many people confuse it with the abortion pill, RU-486. However, Plan B does not work by causing an abortion; it works by preventing ovulation, and it may also prevent a sperm from fertilizing the egg. Sperm can survive in a woman's body up to five days, and conception can occur at any time during that period. If a woman has unprotected sex while she is ovulating, Plan B will not prevent her from becoming pregnant, but if she would otherwise begin ovulating in the next few days, she will be protected.

It is true that copper IUDs and any form of hormonal birth control, including the pill, can change the lining of the womb. This increases the likelihood of miscarriage if the contraceptive functions fail and an egg is fertilized, since it is harder for an embryo to implant in the thinner uterine lining of a woman using an IUD or hormonal contraceptives. How much it increases the likelihood of miscarriage and how often this is likely to happen is difficult to determine, though. Here's why: The body does not begin producing pregnancy hormones until after an embryo is implanted, meaning if there is no implantation, there is no way to know whether an egg has been fertilized. To determine the probability of any given form of contraception causing a miscarriage, scientists would have to come up with some way to determine how often the contraceptive fails to prevent fertilization, factor in the normal levels of embryonic loss (researchers believe two-thirds of embryos fail to develop under normal circumstances[10]), and compare that to the pregnancy rate among women using that form of contraception. Most doctors prefer to just grimace and say, "That *could* happen." Whether it could happen like stubbing your toe, happen like a car accident, or happen like getting struck by lightning is harder to say with any certainty. Some people simply prefer to wear closed-toe shoes, stay off the roads, and avoid electrical storm conditions.

To sum it up, IUDs, the pill, and most other forms of hormonal birth control are contraceptives, not abortifacients, but they may raise the likelihood of early miscarriage if their contraceptive functions fail.

I think that it might be a good idea for us to pause for a moment and take a deep breath before moving on. As I said earlier, these are not easy topics to discuss. They are deeply personal, highly politicized, and (rightly) fraught with emotion. A lot is at stake: the lives of children, the health of women, couples' patterns of sexual intimacy, and how fertility affects career prospects and economic security. We aren't big fans of scientific and ethical uncertainty, and it's tempting to make blanket statements about the rightness or wrongness of certain choices in this realm, even if they aren't strictly true. Many groups and individuals on all sides of this issue have been guilty of spreading inaccuracies that promote their agenda, and sometimes, those inaccuracies have been drilled so deeply into our heads that questioning them feels threatening. But we need to. There is too much at stake to take refuge in comforting half-truths or certainties that are anything but.

Moving forward, talking about contraceptive use, pregnancy, and abortion rates among teenagers isn't going to be easy either. It's one thing to take an unflinching look at the numbers when you are a social scientist. It's quite another when you are a Christian parent, pastor, mentor, or friend who feels overwhelmed by the task of guiding teens toward healthy, God-honoring sexuality in a culture that says anything goes. But facts are our friends, and statistics are a useful way to gauge the social climate we are walking into and prepare accordingly. Looking at the weather app on my phone doesn't bring me any joy when it tells me it is twenty degrees below zero outside. But ignoring my weather app doesn't make it any warmer, and looking at the numbers lets me know I had better pull out the arctic-grade parka and give the minivan several minutes to warm up. Reality can be harsh, but ignoring it does not make it go away—it only makes you unprepared when it sneaks up on you.

Are you ready? Take a deep breath, ask the Holy Spirit to equip you with courage, wisdom, and discernment, and let's dive in.

CONTRACEPTIVE USE, PREGNANCY, AND ABORTION AMONG TEENS

Age is a larger factor in contraceptive use than religious affiliation. Only 82 percent of sexually active fifteen- to nineteen-year-olds in the United States use *any* form of contraception, and many of them rely on less effective methods than their older counterparts do, or methods that require a higher level of consistency to work. Fifty-five percent rely on condoms, 35 percent of sexually active teenage girls are on the pill, and 20 percent rely on their partners to pull out before ejaculation.[11] Am I the only adult who thinks that last strategy is a particularly bad one?

It is hard to get solid numbers on how many adolescents around the world become pregnant, seek abortions, or give birth, as many countries do not track such things. Most North American and European countries do keep records, however, and we can glean a lot from them. Overall, pregnancy and abortion rates have been dropping since the 1990s, and that is a very good thing!

The numbers are a moving target, as social attitudes toward teenage sexuality and access to contraception and abortion shift. Most of the numbers I've used here are from 2011, the last year for which a comprehensive swath of studies is available, and given the pace of change and political shifts of the last decade, it is likely that some of these numbers are already out of date. Still, there is much to be learned from comparing the rates of teen pregnancy and abortion in different countries and considering how culture and policy play into it.

Generally speaking, the countries with the highest teen pregnancy rates also tend to have the lowest abortion rates. This is likely because of a combination of factors: the normalization of teen pregnancy, a more traditional sexual ethic, and less access to both contraception and abortion. Some people find the combination of a more traditional sexual ethic with the normalization of teen pregnancy odd, but here is the thing: teens growing up in more traditional settings have less access to contraceptives and abortions, resulting in more pregnancies carried to term. More pregnancies means less stigma about early-in-life pregnancies, further lowering abortion rates and making young women more ambivalent about contraception.

Among its wealthy, democratic peers, the United States has the highest percentage of teen pregnancies, with 5.7 percent of fifteen- to nineteen-year-olds becoming pregnant. Twenty-six percent of those pregnancies end in abortion. The United Kingdom has a comparatively high rate of teen pregnancies as well, with about 4 percent of fifteen- to nineteen-year-olds becoming pregnant, and approximately 40 percent of those pregnancies being terminated. Fewer than 3 percent of Scandinavian teens become pregnant, but more than half get abortions when they do. Sweden has the highest teen abortion rate on record, at 69 percent, with Denmark close behind. Bear in mind that while numbers like 3 percent and

5.7 percent may not sound all that different from one another on the surface, they mean that American teens are almost twice as likely to get pregnant as teens in Scandinavia.[12]

It is generally agreed that the differences in these numbers have more to do with social attitudes and expectations about sex, contraception, and abortion than with the sexual behavior of teenagers. There is no evidence that teens in Seattle are more sexually active than teens in Stockholm, even if they are four times as likely to become teen parents. It is just that Swedish teens can access contraceptives much more easily than teens in the United States, where birth control exacts a higher social and economic price. When Swedish teens do get pregnant, however, they are far more likely to have an abortion, which costs little to nothing and is generally considered the more socially acceptable choice. Still, the higher pregnancy rate and lower abortion rate means that 0.14 percent of American fifteen- to nineteen-year-olds have abortions, compared to 0.2 percent of their Swedish peers—numbers that are strikingly similar for countries on opposite ends of the spectrum when it comes to abortion rates.

Germany is an interesting case. German statistics are divided at age eighteen instead of twenty, making it difficult to make exact comparisons to other countries, but any way you split it, Germany has one of the lowest teen pregnancy rates in the world. It is similar to its western European neighbors in this: teen pregnancy rates are 1.4 percent in the Netherlands, 2.1 percent in Belgium, and an astonishing 0.8 percent in Switzerland. German statistics fall right in between the Netherlands and Belgium. However, Germany breaks ranks with its EU neighbors when it comes to abortion. In fact, it has a lower abortion rate than the United States, with only

23 percent of teens electing to end their pregnancies.[13] This means that German teens are among the least likely in the developed world to have an abortion: only two out of one thousand underage German girls elect for abortion, and around seven out of one thousand in the under-twenty set.[14] Even if we used the highest numbers available for Germany, German teens are less than half as likely to undergo an abortion as teens in the United States. Why? Probably because while German teens have easy access to contraception and use it at much higher rates than American teens,[15] Germany's abortion laws are quite restrictive. In fact, it remains constitutionally illegal and is difficult to obtain past the first trimester.

LOWERING TEEN PREGNANCY AND ABORTION RATES

It is safe to say that most conscientious adults would like to see a decrease in both pregnancies and abortions among teens. Even the most avid pro-choice crusaders don't typically view abortion as a positive—it's not something people do for fun on a Sunday afternoon. And while attitudes toward teenage sexuality vary widely from place to place and family to family, I don't know a whole lot of adults who are crazy about the idea of teens having sex, either. Some view it as a normal part of the teenage experience, but even those who have no moral qualms about it must acknowledge that it is a risky behavior. The question facing all of us, but particularly those of us who are followers of Christ, is how we can help teens make wise choices about their sexual behavior while keeping our integrity intact, particularly if they are making choices we do not agree with.

In my own evangelical tradition, I think many of our struggles in addressing these issues arise from the fact that we are trying to fight this battle on too many fronts. The objectives tend to be large and amorphous. Prevent teens from having sex. Get the Supreme Court to reverse *Roe v. Wade*. Promote certain forms of sex education in our schools, and oppose others. You know that saying about not being able to see the forest for the trees? It's good to keep the big picture in mind, but if you want to get from one side of the forest to the other, you have to navigate through and around actual trees.

It would be wise for people who are passionate about these issues to become clear on what their primary objective is. Is it to promote celibacy? Lower the teen pregnancy rate? Lower the teen birth rate? Lower the abortion rate? Outlaw abortion? Ironically, while these objectives are in philosophical alignment, they are sometimes at odds with one another on a practical level. It would also be wise for people to give some critical thought to their stance on contraception. How do you feel about contraception, really? Have you used it? How much access should teens be given to different forms of contraception? What hoops do they need to jump through to get it? Who should provide it? Should parental consent be required? Who should pay for it?

I'll show my hand here. I don't want teenagers to have sex. I remained celibate until marriage, and I strongly encourage my own children and the young people in my sphere to do the same. I believe that is the standard God calls us to—celibacy outside of marriage and faithfulness within—and I hold to that standard not because it makes my life better (although it does) or strengthens my relationships (although it does that too), but because I have given my life to Jesus, and am committed to conforming my life to his character and teachings.

However, if teenagers *are* going to have sex, I would much rather they use a safe, highly effective form of contraception. If I had a daughter, I would want her to be able to have a private word with a trusted pediatrician who knew her medical history and had an eye on her overall health— instead of sneaking across town to speak to an unfamiliar practitioner at a women's health clinic. I would want her to have easy access to whatever she needs to lower the risk of an unplanned pregnancy or sexually transmitted infection, regardless of whether I was on board with or even aware of her choices.

Some might consider that a moral compromise, or view the provision of contraception as enabling sex outside of marriage. They are entitled to their opinion. It seems clear to me, however, that this view has led to disastrous outcomes in the United States. How else can we explain the fact that the teen pregnancy rate in the United States is the highest in the developed world and that American teens are almost twice as likely to get an abortion as teens in the freewheeling Netherlands?

When it comes to reproductive health, I would choose lowering teen pregnancy as my primary objective, because it is the fastest and easiest way to save lives and improve outcomes for everyone involved. It doesn't mean that the other outcomes are unimportant, or that we shouldn't be working toward them. It just means that we can stop skimming the forest canopy, distracted by every breeze that rustles the leaves, and focus on forging a path through the trees.

Some will undoubtedly choose different primary objectives. For instance, people with a strong moral objection to contraception may need to set promoting celibacy as their primary objective. This is unlikely to have the same immediate effect on lowering teen pregnancy and abortion as providing free contraception, but it is important to be able to look ourselves in the face at the end of the day and stand before God with a clear conscience. People promoting abstinence-only education also need to grapple with the reality that there are times when celibacy is not an option, and places where young women have precious little choice in the matter. A teenage girl forced into marriage may not be able to protect herself from her husband's advances, but she may be able to protect herself from a pregnancy that her mind, heart, and body are not yet equipped or wanting to carry.

For many Christians, however, the conundrum surrounding these issues has less to do with integrity than it does with a whopping case of ethical ADD that is keeping us distracted and crippling our effectiveness. Whatever primary objective we choose, we should be clear on what it is, why it is important, and how it can best be achieved. And we should base these objectives on solid statistical and scientific evidence, not conjecture and wishful thinking.

HOW TO HELP WHEN YOUNG WOMEN *DO* GET PREGNANT

My church has a shelf full of mismatched coffee mugs, many of them freebies given away at conferences, training events, and volunteer appreciation days. There is one mug that I cannot use, because it sends my blood pressure through the roof. It bears the logo of a Christian school that expelled one of my friends when she became pregnant. She hadn't been attending that school to prepare for Christian leadership, or even because she had a vibrant faith of her own at that point. It was simply the liberal arts school that made the most sense for her and her family at the time—until it became clear that there was no room for pregnant girls at the inn.

Sadly, this is not the only friend this has happened to, or the only school that has chosen law over grace, banishment over embrace. What would people say if unmarried students were allowed to walk around a Christian school obviously pregnant? The tribal school I mentioned at the beginning of this chapter gave girls gift baskets, as a sign of their love and support. Christian schools give girls—well, I won't say it. But we would be wise to consider what messages our institutions are sending to young women who become pregnant and whether those messages bear any resemblance to the one that *Jesus* would like pregnant teens to receive from his people.

Personally, I think Jesus would go with a hug and a "Don't let your heart be troubled. Believe me, I've got you covered. Things may be tough here for a while, but I'm building you a house on my dad's land. You can come live with us, if you want. We are dying to have you and your baby come stay with us!"

Don't you just love Jesus?

What makes these situations even more tragic is that they disrupt young women's education, which is the best buffer against becoming pregnant in the first place, and against poverty when they do become pregnant. This was fleshed out in the chapter about education. Removing a young woman from school is exactly the wrong move if we want positive outcomes for her and the child. And we *are* more concerned about the well-being of mothers and children than of our reputation or donors' opinions, aren't we? If not, maybe we need a "come to Jesus" moment of our own.

Christian schools aren't the only culprits. There are still schools around the world that expel girls for becoming pregnant. And of course getting pregnant and having a child makes it much more difficult for many young women to stay in school and finish their education, wherever they live.

When I met Seline, she was nineteen years old and finishing seventh grade. Married at age fourteen, she was pregnant with her second child when her abusive husband kicked her out. She went to the Ekklesia Foundation for help and didn't miss a beat when the people there asked her what she wanted to do. She wanted to go back to school. It hasn't been an easy road. She has had to entrust her young ones to her mother's care while she was at school, study with students far younger than her, deal with the advances of a teacher whose interest in her was not educational, and depend on financial support from a stranger to cover her expenses. But Seline is determined, and she is finishing her last year of high school as I write this. Her sons, now eight and nine, are getting an education as well. It would have been easier, in the short term, to marry one of the men who expressed interest in her. But Seline has reoriented the trajectory of her life and her family's future, with the help of a literal and metaphorical village that stretches across western Kenya and around the world.

We can help young moms by lobbying the institutions we are involved in to choose grace and embrace over moral distancing and expulsion. Aren't you glad Jesus didn't morally distance himself from us, and expel us from his presence? Sin does need to be addressed, but it should be addressed in a way that brings life and healing, not death and destruction. Pregnant adolescents are not, by and large, predators who are endangering the flock. They are wounded lambs who need help. If we do pluck them from the flock, it should be because we are carrying them in our arms, bringing them to a warm, safe place where they can get better care than we could give them.

We can also help by building and supporting those warm, safe places. Pregnant adolescents need medical care, educational and vocational opportunity, and emotional and practical support, all served up with a lot of love. Where are the places, in your community and around the world, that provide those services?

I was twenty when I got pregnant with my firstborn. My husband and I had been married for several months, and we were excited about the baby. But we were poor and living in a leaky trailer house we had bought for $600, and we were uninsured. I knew the local life care center ran a free clinic a few times a month, so I went there to find out what options I might have. By the time I left their office, I had a trash bag loaded with diapers, baby clothes, and beautiful baby blankets crocheted by a local grandma. While I was there, they had given me everything I needed to get signed up for Medicaid and WIC, and helped me start the process. If I had wanted different housing, they would have helped with that too. The center was a warm, safe place that proactively helped young moms—and any mom, really, who found herself in a tough spot—to access community services and get what they needed to thrive. Maybe there is a place like that in your own community?

Or maybe you yourself could become a warm, safe place. Maybe you offer encouragement with a hug, a meal, or a word of affirmation. Maybe you babysit while Mom is doing college visits, or help her fill out a FAFSA application. Maybe instead of or in addition to sponsoring a child overseas, you sponsor a teenage girl, or donate to schools supporting teen moms. Maybe you weave a prayer into every stitch of the baby blanket you donate to the local crisis pregnancy center.

Or maybe, when you hear people gossiping, you remind them that Jesus was born to a displaced teen mom, and that since whatever we do to "the least of these" we do to Jesus, maybe we should quit talking about Jesus that way. Choosing life is about more than opposing abortion. Choosing life is about committing to thoughts, words, and actions that help everyone flourish.

SEVEN

War and Peace

GIRLS AND CONFLICT

I'm not sure how I knew. Maybe it was the blankets duct-taped over the windows. Maybe some of the words coming through the staticky radio had filtered into my subconscious while I was transitioning from sleep to wakefulness. Maybe it was the expression on my father's face as he fiddled with the radio's knobs, trying to find a better signal. Every fiber of my eight-year-old being knew the answer before the question left my mouth: "Daddy, is there a coup?"

There were a few days of gunfire, a few days of army trucks rumbling past bearing guns and worse cargo, a few days of my baby brother and I being sent to hide in a back room every time a man in uniform approached our house. After the coup had been suppressed and the airport re-opened, my father put my mother, brother, and me on a plane out of Liberia, to stay safe in America until the tensions eased.

My memories of that trip have a dreamlike quality: my four-year-old brother screaming and struggling on the airstrip when he realized our father wasn't coming with us; blonde flight attendants trying to comfort us in Dutch; my mother pounding on the side of the bus we were chasing down on the night-drenched streets of Amsterdam, my brother in one arm and a suitcase in the other; the profound relief that washed over me when I walked down the stairs at my grandparents' house, saw my doll collection nestled in the cradle my uncle Jim had made me, and knew that I was safe. It was Advent when we arrived at my grandparents' house, and to this day, the scent of the anise candy my grandma made every year smells not only of Christmas and home but of a very visceral kind of salvation.

I am completely serious when I say that when I think of dying and going to be with Jesus, I don't imagine hospitals or tunnels of light or pearly gates or loved ones coming to greet me. No, the dazzling dark and light images that disorienting trip seared into my eight-year-old brain are what arise in my mind. If God has a sense of humor, I'll be transported to paradise by cooing blonde angels in pumps and Crayola-blue blazers. What all that says about the cosmic significance of Schiphol International Airport, I will leave to your imagination.

My family was back in Liberia within a few months. But instead of easing, the tensions continued to escalate. We left for good in 1988, and in 1989, civil war broke out, killing a quarter of a million people and displacing a million more over the course of fourteen years. This is a country that only had about four million people to begin with. I spent most of my adolescence worrying about the friends I had left behind in Liberia, with no way of knowing whether they were trapped in Monrovia, or hiding in the bush, or had made the long, dangerous trek to a neighboring country on foot. Whether they had fallen at the end of an assault rifle or machete, or succumbed to starvation or disease.

I was fourteen when my parents broke the news that my best friend and her family had been executed. I locked myself in the bathroom and sobbed, begging God to reverse time and make it not true. When we discovered, a few days later, that we had received bad intelligence and they were all still alive, I considered it a direct answer to a direct prayer, the kind of answer that merited some response from me. When my first son was born six years later, and his hungry cry made my postpartum brain wonder whether my childhood friends had anything to feed the babies they were likely nursing themselves—whether they had enough food to produce breast milk, or were slowly starving alongside their less-resilient children—the form that response would take solidified in my mind. Maybe I couldn't help my friends directly, couldn't track them down, fly into a war zone with a nursing infant strapped to my chest, and deliver tins of tuna and peanut butter and Similac. But I could fight for and alongside them with the only weapons I had at my disposal: the privilege that life and my American passport had unfairly granted me, and my pen.

Most of the issues I have addressed in this book are tightly focused on teen girls. But war affects everyone and everything, from the mightiest man in the province to the microbes in the soil surrounding trees razed in the conflict. War is a broadscale manifestation of human depravity—of our pervasive and unrelenting brokenness—in which the young are sent to die for the misdeeds of the mighty, and in which even those who want to defend life wield weapons of death. I don't care what your ethical stance on war is: just or not, war is humanity's best crack at hell, and we should all be praying for deliverance.

But armed conflict does affect teenage girls in some very particular ways. There are the obvious dangers that everyone living in a war zone faces: the bullets, the bombs, the destruction of homes, and the possibility of displacement. Beyond that, military conflict brings an escalation of many of the issues we have already discussed in this book. Educations are disrupted as schools shut down and people focus on survival. Hospitals are decimated and healthcare systems overrun, making young women more vulnerable to the complications of pregnancy and childbirth. Desperate families who have lost everything in a conflict are more likely to partner off their daughter in order to provide for her, to use the dowry money to care for her siblings, or to get a legal foothold in the country to which they have fled. And sexual violence goes through the roof. The chaos of war, the separation of families, and the destruction of social and civic structures that provided some level of protection in the past make young women from war-torn areas easy targets for predators, to say nothing of the debauched behavior of battle-crazed boys and rape being used as a weapon of war. There are also the phenomena of "bush wives," in which young women are forced into a sexual and domestic union with soldiers; of young women being captured and flat out sold as slaves; of the human sex trafficking that has a tendency to follow military encampments.

One example of this is Fayrouz's story, which ran in a 2016 *Independent* article about how the civil war in Yemen—already an impoverished country with astronomical rates of child marriage and maternal mortality—was affecting girls. In 2014, Fayrouz's future looked promising. She was in school, her father had steady work, and a variety of nonprofits were making a real difference in her community. But then the civil war began, forcing many aid organizations out of the country. Fayrouz's home was bombed, and her family was forced to flee to a camp near a town overrun with refugees. Her mother needed a blood transfusion—the family sold almost everything they had managed to carry with them, but it was still not enough to cover the medical bills. There was nothing left to sell—nothing but eleven-year-old Fayrouz.

No one was happy about the situation. Fayrouz was tiny, not yet four feet tall, and did not have a good grasp of what was going on, but a twenty-five-year-old man had offered a $2,000 dowry for her, with $400 more to be paid later. The elders in the camp made the man sign an agreement that he would not consummate the marriage until she reached puberty, and the wedding went forward in good faith. Fayrouz loved the wedding itself, but when her new husband took her home, began to "flirt" with her, and told her to get into bed, she panicked. She bolted from the room, locked herself in another room, and called her daddy, terrified. Happily, *his* father lived nearby, and Fayrouz's grandfather showed up at the door to collect the little girl. When the article ran, Fayrouz was back in the care of her mother and father, but only until she reached puberty. At that point she would have to be returned to her husband, since there was no way her parents could repay the dowry.

"We needed the money from the dowry," Fayrouz's father explained. "Or else, I would never have married her off." Many other fathers in the refugee camp—even a father who had crusaded against child marriage before the war—described similar situations, marrying off their daughters oldest to youngest in an attempt to keep the other children fed, holding out as long as they could before offering the next girl up to a prospective husband. Others sought marriages for their daughters in an attempt to protect them from the sexual violence stalking the war-torn region or to secure them in a family that had the ability to support them—a family that had plenty of food, and a home with brick walls instead of canvas.[1]

Armed conflict does not have to be officially recognized or sanctioned by a government to be devastating. Honduras is consistently ranked as the most dangerous country in the world to be a woman, in large part because of the anarchy created by gang warfare. This phenomenon made international headlines in 2014, when nineteen-year-old María José Alvarado and her sister Sofía Trinidad were murdered, just days before María was supposed to fly to London to compete in the Miss World pageant. Because of the media coverage, their bodies were recovered and Sofía's boyfriend was charged with the murders. But he was a "powerful man" in Santa Barbara; it was years before the authorities were able to try and convict him.

If the horror had stopped at murder, that would be bad enough, but the reality is much worse. Like many victims and family members in Honduras, María and Sofía's mother and surviving sister spent years living in fear that the man would come after them in retaliation for the trouble the investigation caused him. María Mercedes Bustelo, a district attorney in Honduras, explained that for women, reporting crimes committed against them by gang members is akin to signing their own death warrant. The government can't protect them—the police lack basic resources and can't even enter many neighborhoods without securing military backup.[2] Women's only real options are to stay and pray they survive, living under a constant cloud of terror, or to flee in the hopes that they will be granted asylum elsewhere. They are living in a war zone. But unlike women in recognized war zones, there is no side looking out for their interests, no line they can retreat behind to find safety.

War is brutal and dehumanizing. It can erase decades of progress in the space of days. It is as if war unleashes a beast sleeping inside humanity, or perhaps unleashes a beast *upon* humanity, causing people to do things they could never fathom in times of peace. And the only thing that can truly defeat that beast, once and for all, is the penetrating word of the Lamb who was slain. That word discerns between what is good and what is evil, what is true and what is false, what gives life and what snatches it away.

BARGAINING FOR PEACE

The Bible is full of stories of armed conflict and the impact it has on women. Many of these stories are horrific, proving that humanity hasn't changed much over the past four thousand years. An interesting counter-narrative, however, winds its way through many of these stories: the theme of a woman bargaining for peace, sometimes through extremely unconventional means.

We've already touched on the "certain woman" in Judges 9 who ended Abimelek's reign of terror by dropping a millstone on his head, and the wise woman of Abel Beth Maakah who had the chutzpah to question Joab about his motivations and methods as his men were battering down the city walls. Remember her? You can read her story in 2 Samuel 20:14-22. "Listen, listen!" she cried over the din as a bunch of hardened warriors, armed to the teeth, simultaneously attempted to climb over the walls and knock them down. "Tell Joab to come here so I can speak to him," she said. When she was assured she had the commander's full attention, she asked him what he was about, trying to "swallow up the Lord's inheritance" by destroying a city that was "a mother in Israel"—a place where people had always gone to seek wisdom and guidance. Remember, this is the treacherous dude who had a hand in murdering Abner, and Uriah, and Absalom, and Amasa, and whom even King David was too terrified to challenge. He left that joyous task to his son—David's dying words to Solomon were "Do not let [Joab's] gray head go down to the grave in peace" (1 Kings 2:6), because Joab was a violent man who could not be trusted. Joab was a terror, and the wise woman was confronting him head-on, calling him to account for his actions in her domain.

"Far be it from me to swallow up or destroy!" the would-be swallower-up of the city and destroyer of the walls insisted (2 Samuel 20:20). Joab and the wise woman had a confab and came to an agreement that worked for both of them, although it cost the rebel Sheba his head.

Remember how Rahab insisted that the spies scoping out Jericho spare her and her family if she would hide them from the men who were chasing them (Joshua 2:1-21)? Remember how Abigail prevented David and his men from slaughtering her household by plying them with food, flattery, and allusions to "the staggering burden of needless bloodshed" that David would carry on his conscience if he avenged himself on Nabal's men (1 Samuel 25)? Remember how Esther averted a genocide by throwing a banquet (Esther 7)? Time and time again, a woman's level head prevailed against the passions stirred up by armed conflict, and restored a measure of sanity to men who believed their honor was wrapped up in bloodshed and violence. (Or, alternatively, removed their heads from the equation when they refused to see sense. That happened too.) Men have been making war since the very beginning, and women have been fighting for peace for just as long. It's a gross generalization, of course, but it's also profoundly biblical.

It is also still happening today. In 2011, Leymah Gbowee was awarded the Nobel Peace Prize for her work in organizing the Women of Liberia Mass Action for Peace, sometimes referred to as "the women in white." A mother of five who worked to rehabilitate former child soldiers, Gbowee came to the conclusion that if anything was going to change in her war-torn homeland, the mamas were going to have to take the helm and chart a new course, one that did not involve the destruction of their sons and daughters. The women prayed and sang, organized sit-ins and sex strikes. When they were invited to address the sitting president, Charles Taylor, who was later convicted of war crimes, Gbowee turned from him and directed her words to the only female government official in the room, the president of the Senate. Taylor buckled to their demands and agreed to attend peace talks in Ghana. The women followed him, trapping the warring factions in the meeting room when the talks seemed to be going south. I have seen footage of the event, and there is something deeply satisfying about watching those Liberian mamas swat war-lords who were trying to escape out windows back into the room, yelling that if they were going to act like little boys, they were going to treat them like little boys. Abdulsalami Abubakar, the former president of Nigeria who was presiding over the peace talks, announced that "the peace hall has been seized by General Leymah and her troops." The women of Liberia had had enough, and they weren't going anywhere until the conflict was resolved. The wise women of Liberia took on their Joabs and won.

FIGHTING FOR PEACE

There are many ways to fight for peace. Unfortunately, one of the most popular ways is to impose it by force, a modern-day *Pax Romana* where anyone seeming to disrupt the peace is quickly and brutally dealt with by the dominant powers. This works best for those who happen to look like, think like, speak like, and act like the dominant power group, and who are accepted as members, whoever and whatever that group may be. If you are one of the dissenters challenging the domi-nant culture's idea of peace, or even if you just look like one or are standing too close to one, look out. You may be crucified.

It is hard to overstate how influential this "fighting for peace" model is, not only in wealthy Western countries but around the globe. It often goes hand-in-hand with national-ism and a spoken or unspoken sense of ethnic or cultural su-periority, is buoyed up by ascribing honor to those who meet and enforce its ideals, and is defended by destroying those who don't fit into or affirm its ideals. Of course Hitler and the Nazis come to mind, but what about the British Empire, or Mao's China, or the plight of the Kurds in the Middle East?

This isn't only expressed in military conflict—this happens in the everyday war people wage to maintain dominance. In Duluth, Minnesota, the largest city in my neck of the woods, there is a monument honoring Elias Clayton, Elmer Jackson, and Isaac McGhie, black carnival workers who were falsely accused of raping a woman in 1920, and were dragged out of jail and lynched. Clayton, Jackson, and McGhie were murdered because they didn't look like the dominant group and challenged their racial dominance. Their very existence was perceived as a threat, and like so many black men throughout U.S. history, they were killed to send the message that black people were just barely tolerated, and had better act beaten and afraid.

This was the second lynching to take place in Duluth. The first victim was Olli Kinkkonen, an immigrant opposed to World War I who had renounced his U.S. citizenship to avoid being sent to fight. He was dragged from his boarding house, tarred and feathered to send a message to pacifists, and hanged just outside the city in 1918. Kinkkonen was murdered because, like many Finnish Americans of his day, he didn't think like the dominant group and thus challenged their cultural dominance. He insulted them by refusing to affirm their actions, don their uniform, and enforce their ideals, and was killed as a result.

Unsurprisingly, no one was charged in any of those deaths, although three men served time for rioting in connection with the lynching of Clayton, Jackson, and McGhie. That's right—they went to jail for disturbing the peace, not for murdering three men. Kinkkonen's death was conveniently ruled a suicide, although precious few Duluthians have ever believed that, and the region's tight-knit community of Finnish immigrants got the message his killers were sending loud and clear.

It is interesting to note that Kinkkonen was killed for much the same reason that the early Christian martyrs were killed by the Roman Empire. It wasn't that Christians were part of a disenfranchised ethnic group—they came from a variety of backgrounds, and the Romans weren't that tied up about race. It wasn't that Romans had it in for Christian doctrine—the Romans typically let people worship as they wanted, as long as they paid homage to the emperor as well. No—Christians were considered a threat because they were disrupting the social order. Their refusal to participate in civic events like gladiatorial matches was considered an insult to the culture, and their refusal to offer even a nominal, I-don't-really-believe-this-but-will-do-it-to-avoid-rocking-the-boat sacrifice to the gods was perceived as their refusing to do their part to ensure national security. It's a gross simplification, but the early Christian martyrs were, by and large, killed for being unpatriotic.

Why am I talking about this in a book about empowering young women? I am talking about it because all too often, the hubris of nationalism and ethnic superiority is the fuel that feeds military conflict (and many other sorts of conflict) and is the barrier that prevents us from helping those caught in the crossfire. Here's a hard truth. The gospel doesn't leave any room for an "us first" mindset, or even an "us and them" mindset, particularly when we are talking about brothers and sisters in Christ. The gospel is not only unpatriotic, tearing down the walls we've built to delineate ourselves from our fellow human beings. The gospel is blisteringly impractical, calling us to lay ourselves down for the benefit of others, even those we consider exceedingly "other."

Don't get me wrong—there is nothing wrong with celebrating what is good and God-honoring about the nation in which you live. But our allegiance belongs to Jesus and his kingdom, and that kingdom has no regard for gender, ethnicity, nationality, or class distinctions. In fact, I would go so far as to say that Christians owe no less to their brothers and sisters on the other side of the planet than they do to their brothers and sisters on the other side of the province.

We do, however, owe a particular debt to the people we live with, work with, interact with, or turn away from every day: the individuals whom God in his wisdom has placed in our paths.

FOREIGNERS, ORPHANS, AND WIDOWS

She wouldn't let go of my hand. I was sitting on the floor at the feet of an impossibly tiny old woman swathed in black, whose age had procured her a pride of place on a rickety metal folding chair. She apologized for her English as she translated a few paragraphs of Arabic text into words I could understand. Her son's English was better, she said, but he was legally blind, and wouldn't be able to read it. He had been a college professor back in Baghdad, years ago before they were forced to flee, but he was unable to work in the United States. The two of them had just been resettled in their new apartment, in an entirely new community, the previous day, but she wanted to invite me over for dinner—to share her food, her story, her language, and out of love, her faith.

It was an impulse I recognized—the same impulse that had drawn me to the tiny, huddled woman in the first place.

To this day, I regret that I didn't follow through on my instinct to invite her and her son to Thanksgiving dinner at my house; that I didn't dial the number she had given me to set up a time to visit her apartment. I can't help but feel that I missed out on something special, an amazing opportunity God wrapped up like a gift and presented to me with a flourish. It makes me sad.

There's not a lot most of us can do about armed conflict, particularly when it happens in other parts of the world. There are *some* things we can do, of course. We can pray for peace, lobby for better policies, volunteer with peacemaking organizations. My children's pediatrician spent a tour of duty patching people up in Iraq, including a thirteen-year-old girl who desperately needed a pediatrician, and I have a few friends who are active in conflict resolution between historic enemies. But for the most part, African warlords, Central American gang leaders, and Western heads of state don't care what some pastor in Missouri, or church in California, or parent in Saskatchewan thinks about their practices. We should do our level best to bargain for peace, but as followers of Jesus, we should also commit to attending to the wounds created by armed conflict.

Perhaps the most practical way we can help young women (and anyone) caught in the crossfire of conflict is to help those who have been displaced, particularly the ones who have shown up on our doorstep looking for help. The refugee. The immigrant. Those for whom home became so dangerous that they were willing to leave everything behind, brave oceans and deserts and overcrowded camps and unfriendly policies, to live as a stranger in a strange land.

The Bible leaves no question about how we are to treat foreigners seeking refuge inside our borders: we are to remember our own immigrant history, remember how God rescued us from bondage and oppression, and look after them. In Deuteronomy 26, the Hebrew people were taught to recite a familiar prayer when they brought their firstfruits to the temple: "My father was a wandering Aramean . . ." This was followed by an acknowledgment that they owed everything to God, who had seen their misery and delivered them, and that they were giving a tenth of their crops not just to the Levites who served in the tabernacle, but to "the foreigner, the fatherless and the widow, according to all you commanded." The people were further instructed to pray, "I have not turned aside from your commands nor have I forgotten any of them" (Deuteronomy 26:13).

Oh church. Sometimes I fear that we could not say that prayer with integrity. And the irony that so many displaced people at the time I was writing this book are *actual* wandering Arameans—Syrians and Iraqis fleeing the homeland they share in common with Father Abraham—feels like a mockery of the faith we purport. I am never sure how to respond when Christians stand in opposition to immigration. Welcoming strangers isn't practical, I know. Trust me, this foster mom knows. It is hard. It is uncomfortable. It can feel like a threat to the things we hold most dear. But I take the words of Jesus very seriously, and when he says that whatever we do to the hungry, the thirsty, the sick and imprisoned and naked, and yes, the stranger, we do to him (Matthew 25:40)—well, I believe him.

I can almost feel people's toes crunching under my feet as I write this, but I love Jesus and his church too much to water this down. Jesus said we will be judged according to how we treat the least of these. That our actions in this area speak louder than our words and show where our true allegiances lie. Friends, Jesus never called us to be comfortable. He called us to pick up our crosses and lay our lives down. He wasn't kidding. He wasn't even using hyperbole. He did exactly that himself. Is the servant better than the master? Did Jesus make that torturous climb to Calvary so we could coast through our lives while the world burns around us, consuming the vulnerable stretching their hands out for help?

No. No, he did not. And we, as his people, have got to do better.

So how can we help girls from war-torn areas, their families, and the strangers that conflict has chased to our shores? Here are a few ideas.

Make your voice heard. I suspect that most people reading this book have something many can only dream about: a real voice in their government. We can vote. We can push for good policies. We may even be able to run for office ourselves, calling attention to important issues even if we don't win. We have ways to make our wishes known, our values understood, and our voices heard, with the expectation that our leaders will listen.

I've never been one to call or write letters to my political representatives, but when I heard about a new immigration policy of separating children from their families at the U.S. border, I opened up my email and started typing. I explained that as a foster mom who is familiar with the trauma that family separation creates—not to mention the overrun and underfunded state of child protection agencies in the United States—I was deeply concerned. I told my very conservative senator that the plan was not only unethical; it was fiscally irresponsible. I pleaded with my very liberal senator to make reform in this area an urgent priority. I reminded the congressman who represents my district of the deep, lingering scars that the policy of removing Native American children from their families and placing them in boarding schools had created in our communities, and pointed out the tragic irony that we were once again separating the Indigenous children of this continent from their families. I don't know how much impact my individual letters had, but I do know that a politically diverse nation of outraged mama bears rising up and snarling at their representatives caused many to start backpedaling. The damage that policy has wrought has not been undone yet, and may never be fully undone in this life. But how much worse would it have been if people *hadn't* spoken out against it? Politics is a messy business, and I understand the impulse to stay out of it, but maybe, just maybe, God is calling you to speak up.

Donate. Imagine for a minute that your hometown is under siege. You worked at a small construction business, but no one is building in a war zone, and the owners left town when it became apparent that things were going downhill. Your wife took some extra shifts at a café downtown to make up some of the lost income, but the city is flooded with men from out of town, and you are terrified for her safety. You have taken to driving your children to school instead of letting them walk, burning precious fuel, but you saw the way the soldiers looked at your teenage daughter, even with you right there, and you don't want her on the streets alone. You are almost to the end of your meager savings when mortar fire hits your apartment. Miraculously, your whole family emerges from the rubble, but precious little else was spared. The old car you saved so long to buy was destroyed. With the fighting closing in, you gather your family, grab everything you can carry on your back, and begin the trek toward the nearest refugee settlement.

How are you going to keep your family clothed, and sheltered, and fed? Your daughter was on track to get into college, the first person in your family to do so. Will she be able to finish her last two years of high school—and even if there is a school at the camp, will it be good enough to get her into the university? What if your son's asthma flares up, or your wife tells you there is another little one on the way? You have always taken pride in your work, but with everything that you have worked for gone, how will your family make it until you are able to get back on your feet? Will they even allow you to get a job in the country you are fleeing to?

Refugees need financial support, and there are numerous organizations committed to helping them with short-term and long-term needs. The Red Cross. World Relief. The International Rescue Committee. Oxfam. Perhaps your church or denomination has a special fund for refugees. The ancient Hebrews gave a portion of the firstfruits not only for the maintenance of the tabernacle and the Levites who ran it; they gave to care for the needs of those who were truly desperate and unable to support themselves. Maybe we should allocate a portion of our giving that way as well.

Go out for lunch. "I wanted to come to America because of the opportunity." I was attending a dinner at my parents' church and sitting by a family who had recently come from Syria. The man had been a shop owner in Aleppo. When he took a bullet to the arm, he knew his young family had to get out if they wanted to survive. They had spent years in a camp, waiting to be resettled, and his wife gave birth to their two youngest children there.

It takes guts to leave the only place you've ever known and build a life in a new land, and many of those who do so are industrious and entrepreneurial. Many of our neighborhoods are dotted with small businesses run by people who came to these shores as refugees. Why not shop there? Try out an African place for lunch, buy your fruit and vegetables at the Central American market down the street, pick up baklava from a Middle Eastern bakery when it's your turn to provide treats at the office, and tank up at an immigrant-owned gas station. It's a practical, dignified way to help newcomers get a financial foothold, and there is a high likelihood that some of the dollars you spend there will be sent back to help loved ones in less fortunate circumstances.

Be a good neighbor. A couple of years ago, my friend Catherine told me that most immigrants living in the United States are never invited into a native-born American's home. I was stunned. No dinner invitations. No birthday parties. No backyard barbecues. No giggly sleepovers. Aren't we inviting the international students studying at our universities home for the holidays? Aren't we encouraging our teens to reach out to the new students showing up at their high school, nervous, uncertain, and pining for home? Apparently not—or at least not enough.

This one is simple, folks. We just need to be more intentional about being good neighbors. Smile at people. Invite them over for coffee. Show up for cultural events happening in your community. Volunteer to be an English tutor at your local library. If there is a refugee resettlement agency in your area, call them up and see if they need donations, or help painting an apartment, or drivers who can help people run errands until they get their license. Just normal stuff—the stuff you would do for a friend or relative if they were moving to your neighborhood and needed a bit of help getting settled. This won't only help them—it will enrich your own life in incredible ways. We all need friends. Widen your circles a bit, and watch what God does.

Another way to fight for peace. Earlier in this chapter, we talked about one of the most common ways people "fight for peace": attempting to reduce conflict by forcing others to think, speak, and act in lockstep with the dominant powers, and resorting to violence when people step out of line or don't fit in the line in the first place. But that isn't true peace, even if it does promote social stability for a certain group of people. That is oppression. And operating from that mindset will not help us reach out to the people God wants us to reach out to. It teaches us to fear those who are different and to lash out against those we perceive as a threat to our way of life.

But there is another way to fight for peace. A way of invitation, not annihilation. In Ephesians, the apostle Paul reminds us that our struggle is not against flesh and blood—not against other human beings—but against "the spiritual forces of evil in the heavenly realms. Therefore put on the full armor of God, so that when the day of evil comes, you may be able to stand your ground, and after you have done everything, to stand" (Ephesians 6:12-13). We can't truly impose peace through violence or righteousness through oppression. We can't beat the enemy at his own game, and we certainly can't win playing by his rules. We only become more like him, allowing ourselves to be made over in his image as we give in to fear and choose self-preservation over reconciliation. As we choose the status quo over true shalom.

No, the only way we can really win is to refuse to play the enemy's game, and live as stalwart citizens of the kingdom of heaven—citizens who have pledged our allegiance to the crucified Lamb and ordered our lives according to his principles. We win when we share the amazing news that whatever happens, we don't have to be afraid, because Jesus came to set us free, and we don't have to live as slaves to sin and death anymore. We don't win by destroying our enemies. We win by calling them back to life so that they become brothers, sisters, and friends. That is what true peace, shalom, looks like: not the absence of conflict, but the presence of reconciliation. And that, my friends, is very good news.

Epilogue

Shalom, the biblical concept of peace, is not so much about the absence of conflict as about a state of being in which things are rightly ordered and able to flourish. Shalom is a balanced ledger, a misunderstanding that has been cleared up, both of your favorite woolen socks miraculously emerging from the dryer and being available on that cold, wet day when you need them.

And it's not just a state of being. Shalom can be used as a verb, meaning it's something you can *do* to someone or something. Stole a jump rope from Target when you were ten? Shalom them by paying it off. One of your tires a little low? Shalom your car by airing it up. Inadvertently started a rumor that hurt your friend? Shalom her by telling the truth and making amends.

Live in a world where young women are routinely aborted, abandoned, abused, neglected, and sexualized? Where they lack access to education and healthcare, are partnered off before they are old enough to decide for themselves, and where their tenuous futures are often crushed and cut short by the wheels of war? Shalom, my friend. Shalom. And by that I don't mean be at peace with the situation. I mean don the full armor of God, gather up every shred of courage and moral fortitude and righteous indignation you have amassed over your years on this earth, and fight to make this world a safer, better place for our girls. A place where they can have shalom.

I have painted this book in the broadest of brushstrokes, using the colors and textures God put on my palette. There is so much more that could and should be said, and so much more that has been said, by people diving deeper into these issues than I had the time, space, or expertise to go. How does racial injustice play into each of these problems? What are girls' prospects when it comes to gender parity in the workplace and in politics? How might climate change affect young women growing up in agrarian communities? How can the church best advocate for better treatment of women and girls among people who are *not* followers of Jesus, and who may be coming from a very different cultural and religious worldview?

There are so many different issues to be explored, problems to be tackled, and solutions to be unearthed. None of us can address all of them. But that is why God instituted the church, a global network of one anothers who have been called and equipped to operate as Christ's body here on earth. I suspect that one or two of the issues we have touched on over the course of this book—or maybe an issue we did *not* talk about, that seemed glaringly absent—may have made you angry, or may have sparked your interest, or is weighing particularly heavy on your heart. Pay attention to that! The Holy Spirit may be trying to direct your steps.

So consider this your invitation to jump into the fray and fight for shalom for girls. Every voice, every heart, every set of hands is needed. Gather your people, gather your resources, and resist until the powers, principalities, and dominant forces of this world have been trampled under your feet. Don't just fight to win; fight because we bear the name of Christ and surrendering to sin is not an option, no matter how hard and hopeless the battle may seem at times. God does not want his daughters to be abused and oppressed, crushed under violent systems that put certain forms of human life above others. God wants all of us, female and male, to flourish together, as radiant image-bearers who reflect God's glory to the world.

Fight on, my friends, and flourish. Shalom.

ACKNOWLEDGMENTS

Why do acknowledgments always come at the end of the book, when the reader is almost as tired of reading it as the author is of writing it? It is a question for the ages, but I'm gonna push through the carpal tunnel and keep going, because there are some people I need to thank.

Aaron Armstrong and Valerie Weaver-Zercher. It is not often that authors thank their husband and their editor on the same line, but in this case, I think it is merited. Both of you have exhibited the patience of Job over this past year while I juggled work, parenting teens, grad school, and this project. Thanks for sticking with me, even when I was going a little bit (okay, a lotta bit) nuts!

Jamison, Clay, Carter, and Grant, I love you to pieces, and am *so thankful* for all the ways you have flexed and flowed over this past year. You are amazing. I owe you so much Dairy Queen this summer!

To the women of the Redbud Writers Guild, who prayed this book into being, and the sisters at St. Scholastica, who let me run away to their monastery when I needed time to pray, cry, and focus—thank you. I don't think I could have done this without you.

Huge thanks to my agent, Rachel Kent, who made me add more stories. You were right!

To the legion of people who have loved me well and stood in the gap for me this past year, thank you. I am so, so thankful for each and every one of you.

NOTES

Chapter 1

1 Nicholas Kristof and Sheryl WuDunn, *Half the Sky* (New York: Alfred A. Knopf, 2009), xvii.

2 United Nations Population Fund, *Report of the International Workshop on Skewed Sex Ratios at Birth* (New York: UNFPA, 2011).

3 United Nations, Department of Economic and Social Affairs, Population Division, *Sex Differentials in Childhood Mortality* (New York: United Nations, 2011).

Chapter 2

1 George Psacharopoulos and Harry Anthony Patrinos, "Returns to Investment in Education: A Further Update" (Washington, DC: World Bank, 2002).

2 Chris Fortson, "Women's Rights Vital for Developing World," *Yale News Daily*, February 14, 2003.

3 "Child Marriage," UNICEF, March 2018, https://data.unicef.org/topic/child-protection/child-marriage/.

4 Ibid.

5 United Nations Population Fund, *State of the World's Population, 1990* (New York: UNFPA, 1990).

6 Betty Hart and Todd R. Risley, "The Early Catastrophe: The 30 Million Word Gap by Age 3," *American Educator* 27, no. 1 (Spring 2003): 4–9.

7 Ayesha B. M. Kharsany and Quarraisha A. Karin, "HIV Infection and AIDS in Sub-Saharan Africa: Current Status, Challenges, and Opportunities," *Open AIDS Journal* 10 (2016): 34–48.

8 Global Coalition on Women and AIDS, *Educate Girls, Fight AIDS*, Issues Brief 1 (Washington, DC: UNAIDS, 2005), 1.

9 Jerusalem Torah *Sotah* 3:4 (19a).

10 Dorothy Sayers, *Are Women Human?* (Grand Rapids, MI: Eerdmans, 1971), 47.

11 Richard M. Kavuma, "Free Universal Secondary Education in Uganda Has Yielded Mixed Results," *Poverty Matters* (blog), *The Guardian*, October 25, 2011, https://www.theguardian.com/global-development/poverty-matters/2011/oct/25/free-secondary-education-uganda-mixed-results.

12 Nikole Hannah-Jones, "The Problem We All Live With," part 1, *This American Life*, July 31, 2015.

13 Christopher S. Rugaber, "Pay Gap between College Grads and Everyone Else at a Record," Associated Press, January 12, 2017.

14 Anup Shah, "Poverty Facts and Stats," *Global Issues*, last modified January 17, 2013, www.globalissues.org/article/26/poverty-facts-and-stats.

15 Puja Changoiwala, "Why India's Widespread Period Shaming Must End," *Self*, September 25, 2017, https://www.self.com/story/indias-period-shaming-must-end.

16 Rashmi Verma, "About 23 Percent Girls Drop Out of School on Reaching Puberty," *Down to Earth*, last modified January 22, 2018, https://www.downtoearth.org.in/blog/health/23-girls-drop-out-of-school-on-reaching-puberty-59496.

17 Tharanga Yakupitiyage, "Menstrual Hygiene Gaps Continue to Keep Girls from School," *Inter Press Service*, May 27, 2016, http://www.ipsnews.net/2016/05/menstrual-hygiene-gaps-continue-to-keep-girls-from-school/.

18 "Labor Force, Female," The World Bank, September 2018, https://data.worldbank.org/indicator/sl.tlf.totl.fe.zs.

19 United Nations, Department of Economic and Social Affairs, Statistics Division, "Work," chap. 4 in *The World's Women 2015: Trends and Statistics* (New York: United Nations, 2015), https://unstats.un.org/unsd/gender/chapter4/chapter4.html.

Chapter 3

1 "The Common Sense Census: Media Use by Tweens and Tweens," Common Sense Media, November 2015, https://www.commonsensemedia.org/the-common-sense-census-media-use-by-tweens-and-teens-infographic.

2 Jean Twenge, "Teens Are Sleeping Less—but There's a Surprisingly Easy Fix," *The Conversation*, October 2017, https://theconversation.com/teens-are-sleeping-less-but-theres-a-surprisingly-easy-fix-85157.

3 Michael B. Robb, Willow Bay, and Tina Vennegaard, *The New Normal: Parents, Teens, and Digital Devices in Japan* (San Francisco: Common Sense, 2017); "Social Networking Is Tops for Kids in Brazil," eMarketer,

October 2014, https://www.emarketer.com/Article/Social-Network-ing-Tops-Kids-Brazil/1013105.

4 Bureau of Economic and Business Affairs, "2013 Investment Climate Statement—Sierra Leone," U.S. Department of State, March 2013, https://www.state.gov/e/eb/rls/othr/ics/2013/204729.htm; Annabelle Wittels and Nick Maybanks, *Communication in Sierra Leone: An Analysis of Media and Mobile Audiences* (London: BBC Media Action, 2016).

5 Anonymous, comment on anonymous, "If someone from the 1950s . . . ," Reddit, https://as.reddit.com/r/AskReddit/comments/15yaap/if_someone_from_the_1950s_suddenly_appeared_today/c7qyp13/.

6 Tara Bahrampour, "Teens Who Spend Less Time in Front of a Screen Are Happier—Up to a Point, New Research Shows," *Washington Post*, January 22, 2018, https://www.washingtonpost.com/news/inspired-life/wp/2018/01/22/teens-who-spend-less-time-in-front-of-screens-are-happier-up-to-a-point-new-research-shows/?utm_term=.61e3cda16779.

7 Jean Twenge, "Teenage Depression and Suicide Are Way Up—and So Is Smartphone Use," *Washington Post*, November 19, 2017, https://www.washingtonpost.com/national/health-science/teenage-depression-and-suicide-are-way-up--and-so-is-smartphone-use/2017/11/17/624641ea-ca13-11e7-8321-481fd63f174d_story.html?utm_term=.f5f46a30fb4c.

8 Jean M. Twenge et al., "Increases in Depressive Symptoms, Suicide-Related Outcomes, and Suicide Rates among U.S. Adolescents after 2010 and Links to Increased New Media Screen Time," *Clinical Psychological Science* 6, no. 1 (November 2017): 3–17.

9 Samantha Cole, "Study of 500,000 Teens Suggests Association between Excessive Screen Time and Depression," *Motherboard*, November 17, 2017, https://motherboard.vice.com/en_us/article/mb3nbx/study-of-teenagers-suggests-association-between-excessive-screen-time-and-depression.

10 "The Common Sense Census."

11 Royal Society for Public Health, *#StatusOfMind: Social Media and Young People's Mental Health and Well-Being* (London: Royal Society for Public Health, 2018), 8.

12 Nancy Jo Sales, *American Girls* (New York: Alfred A. Knopf, 2016), 18.

13 "The Common Sense Census."

14 Rebecca Greenfield, "Silicon Valley Is a Big Ole Fraternity," *The Atlantic*, April 27, 2012, https://www.theatlantic.com/technology/archive/2012/04/silicon-valley-big-ole-fraternity/328778/.

15 Sales, *American Girls*, 53, 59–60.

16 J. Cheryl Exum, "The Song of Solomon," in *The New Oxford Annotated Bible* (New York: Oxford University Press, 2010), 952.

Chapter 4

1 Eugene Cho, "The Oldest Injustice in Human History Is the Way We Treat Women," accessed October 22, 2018, https://eugenecho.com/2008/11/29/the-oldest-injustice-in-human-history/.

2 Alana Vagianos, "30 Shocking Domestic Violence Statistics That Remind Us It's an Epidemic," *Huffington Post*, last modified December 6, 2017, https://www.huffingtonpost.com/2014/10/23/domestic-violence-statistics_n_5959776.html.

3 National Center for Injury Prevention and Control, "Findings from the National Intimate Partner and Sexual Violence Survey," Centers for Disease Control, accessed October 22, 2018, https://www.cdc.gov/violenceprevention/pdf/NISVS-StateReportFactsheet.pdf.

4 David Finkelhor et al., "The Lifetime Prevalence of Child Sexual Abuse and Sexual Assault Assessed in Late Adolescence," *Journal of Adolescent Health* 55, no. 3 (September 2014): 329–33.

5 Matthew Breiding et al., *Prevalence and Characteristics of Sexual Violence, Stalking, and Intimate Partner Violence Victimization—National Intimate Partner and Sexual Violence Survey, United States, 2011* (Atlanta: Centers for Disease Control, 2014).

6 Sherry Hamby et al., *Children's Exposure to Intimate Partner Violence and Other Family Violence* (Washington, DC: U.S. Department of Justice, 2011).

7 "10 Startling Statistics about Children of Domestic Violence," Childhood Domestic Violence Association, last modified February 21, 2014, https://cdv.org/2014/02/10-startling-domestic-violence-statistics-for-children/.

8 UNICEF, *Behind Closed Doors: The Impact of Domestic Violence on Children* (West Sussex: The Body Shop International, 2006).

9 "Men's Nonviolence Classes," Domestic Abuse Intervention Programs, accessed October 22, 2018, https://www.theduluthmodel.org/about-us/mens-nonviolence-classes/.

10 J. Lee Grady, "Jael's Lethal Weapon: Why Women Cannot Be Sidelined in This Critical Hour," address, Christians for Biblical Equality, July 2013, Pittsburgh, PA, https://www.cbeinternational.org/resources/recording-video/jaels-lethal-weapon-why-women-cannot-be-sidelined-critical-hour.

Chapter 5

1 Matthew Bramlett and Wayne Mosher, *Cohabitation, Marriage, Divorce, and Remarriage in the United States*, Vital Health Statistics 23, no. 22 (Washington, DC: National Center for Health Statistics, 2002), 18.

2 Ibid., 16.

3 Gladys Martinez and Joyce Abma, *Sexual Activity, Contraceptive Use, and Childbearing of Teenagers Aged 15–19 in the United States*, NCHS Data Brief 209 (Washington, DC: National Center for Health Statistics, 2015).

4 Joyce Martin et al., *Births: Final Data for 2016*, National Vital Statistics Reports 67, no. 1 (Washington, DC: National Center for Health Statistics, 2018), 6.

5 Carmen Solomon-Fears, *Nonmarital Births: An Overview* (Washington, DC: Congressional Research Service, July 30, 2014).

6 Kelleen Kaye, Katherine Sullentrop, and Corinna Sloup, *The Fog Zone: How Misperceptions, Magical Thinking, and Ambivalence Put Young Adults at Risk for Unplanned Pregnancy* (Washington, DC: National Campaign to Prevent Teen and Unplanned Pregnancy, 2009).

7 Chris Baynes, "More Than 200,000 Children Married in the U.S. over the Last 15 Years," *The Independent*, July 8, 2017, https://www.independent .co.uk/news/world/americas/200000-children-married-us-15-years-child -marriage-child-brides-new-jersey-chris-christie-a7830266.html.

8 "Child Marriage," UNICEF, March 2018, https://data.unicef.org/topic/ child-protection/child-marriage/.

9 UNICEF, *The State of the World's Children 2016: A Fair Chance for Every Child* (New York: UNICEF, 2016).

10 Gabrielle Moss, "The Average Age Women Got Their First Period, throughout History," *Bustle*, October 2, 2015, https://www.bustle.com/ articles/114490-the-average-age-women-got-their-first-period -throughout-history.

11 Theresa Scholl, "Puberty and Adolescent Pregnancy," in *Women and Health*, eds. Marlene Goldman and Maureen Hatch (San Diego: Academic Press, 2000), 90.

12 Moss, "The Average Age Women."

13 Michael Best, "The Age of Marriage," Internet Shakespeare Editions, accessed November 29, 2018, http://internetshakespeare.uvic.ca/m/ lifetimes/society/family/marriage.html.

14 United States Census Bureau, "Median Age at First Marriage, 1890 to Present," accessed November 29, 2018, https://www.census.gov/content/ dam/Census/library/visualizations/time-series/demo/families-and -households/ms-2.pdf.

15 United Nations Population Fund, *State of the World's Population, 1990* (New York: UNFPA, 1990).

Chapter 6
1 Save the Children, *State of the World's Mothers 2014* (Fairfield, CT: Save the Children, 2014).

2 Ibid.

3 Ibid.

4 Nicholas Kristof, "A Tipping Point on Maternal Mortality?" *On the Ground* (blog), *New York Times*, July 30, 2009, https://kristof.blogs .nytimes.com/2009/07/30/a-tipping-point-on-maternal-mortality/.

5 J. Cheryl Exum, "'Mother in Israel': A Familiar Figure Reconsidered," in *Feminist Interpretation of the Bible*, ed. Letty Russell (Louisville: West-minster John Knox Press, 1985), 74.

6 Stephanie Busari, "'Don't Use Birth Control,' Tanzania's President Tells Women in the Country," CNN, September 11, 2018, https://www.cnn.com/2018/09/11/africa/tanzania-birth-control-magufuli-intl/index.html.

7 United Nations, *World Family Planning 2017 Highlights* (New York: United Nations, 2017), 6.

8 Jo Jones, William Mosher, and Kimberly Daniels, *Current Contraceptive Use in the United States, 2006–2010, and Changes in Patterns of Use since 1995, National Health Statistics Report*, no. 60 (Hyattsville, MD: National Center for Health Statistics, 2012), 1.

9 Rachel Jones and Joerg Dreweke, *Countering Conventional Wisdom: New Evidence on Religion and Contraceptive Use* (New York: Guttmacher Institute, 2011).

10 Krista Conger, "Earlier, More Accurate Prediction of Embryo Survival Enabled by Research," Stanford Medicine News Center, October 3, 2010, https://med.stanford.edu/news/all-news/2010/10/earlier-more-accurate -prediction-of-embryo-survival-enabled-by-research.html.

11 Laura Lindberg, John Santelli, and Sheila Desai, "Understanding the Decline in Adolescent Fertility in the United States, 2007–2012," *Journal of Adolescent Health* 59, no. 5 (2016): 577–83.

12 Gilda Sedgh et al., "Adolescent Pregnancy, Birth, and Abortion Rates across Countries: Levels and Recent Trends," *Journal of Adolescent Health* 56, no. 2 (2015): 223–30.

13 Ibid.

14 On abortions among underage girls in Germany, ibid.; on abortions among women under twenty, Advocates for Youth, "Adolescent Sexual Health in Europe and the United States: The Case for a Rights. Respect. Responsibility. Approach," accessed October 29, 2018, https://www .advocatesforyouth.org/storage/advfy/documents/adolescent_sexual_ health_in_europe_and_the_united_states.pdf.

15 Advocates for Youth, "Adolescent Sexual Health."

Chapter 7

1 Sudarsan Raghavan, "Yemen War: The Girl Forced to Marry at 11 Whose Story Exposes the Conflict's Toll on Children," *The Independent*,

July 7, 2016, https://www.independent.co.uk/news/world/middle-east/
yemen-war-the-girl-forced-to-marry-at-11-whose-story-exposes-the
-conflicts-toll-on-children-a7125151.html.
2 Juju Chang et al., "'Men Can Do Anything They Want to Women in
Honduras': Inside One of the Most Dangerous Places on Earth to Be a
Woman," ABC News, May 3, 2017, https://abcnews.go.com/International/
men-women-honduras-inside-dangerous-places-earth-woman/
story?id=47135328.

THE AUTHOR

Jenny Rae Armstrong is an award-winning writer and pastor at Darrow Road Wesleyan Church in Superior, Wisconsin. Her work has appeared in dozens of publications, including *Today's Christian Woman*, *Relevant*, *Mutuality*, and *Red Letter Christians*, and her articles on gender justice and empowering women and girls have won three Evangelical Press Association awards and two Associated Church Press awards. She is the author of *Don't Hide Your Light Under a Laundry Basket* and a youth curriculum, *Called Out!* Armstrong has degrees from the University of Northwestern and North Park Theological Seminary. *Covenant Companion* recognized her as one of the Evangelical Covenant Church's "40 under 40." Armstrong lives in northern Wisconsin with her husband, Aaron, and their kids. Connect with her at JennyRaeArmstrong.com.